D0679813

SHARES

TRUST COMPANY

THE PROVINCE OF ONTARIO

CUSIP 926106 10 5

fully paid and
in the

PAR VALUE OF $1.00 EACH

ransferable on the books of the Company by the holder
er of this certificate properly endorsed. This certificate
the Company or by a Transfer Agent of the Company.
rate to be signed by its duly authorized officers.

SPECIMEN

President

LINDSAY OR TORONTO

THE MONEY LABYRINTH

THE
MONEY
LABYRINTH

A Stock Market Guide
by a Canadian Broker

S.E. Woods

1984
Doubleday Canada Limited, Toronto, Canada
Doubleday & Company, Inc., Garden City, New York

Library of Congress Catalog Card Number 84-12103
ISBN: 0-385-19651-2
Copyright © 1984 by Shirley E. Woods
First edition
Jacket design by David Wyman
Interior design by Irene Carefoot
Printed and bound in Canada by T.H. Best Printing Company Limited
Typesetting by ART-U Graphics Ltd.

Canadian Cataloguing in Publication Data

Woods, Shirley E.
   The money labyrinth : a stock market guide by a
Canadian broker

Includes index.
ISBN 0-385-19651-2

1. Investments — Canada. I. Title.

HG5152.W66 1984   332'.0415'0971   C84-098786-2

Library of Congress Cataloging in Publication Data

Woods, Shirley E.
   The money labyrinth.

   Includes index.
   1. Investments — Canada — Handbooks, manuals, etc.
I. Title.
HG5154.W66 1984   332.63'2'0971   84-12103
ISBN 0-385-19651-2

This book is affectionately dedicated to my clients, with the hope that they will be as tolerant in the future as they have been in the past.

Contents

PREFACE

YOU WOULDN'T PLAY high stakes poker with a bunch of card sharks unless you were an expert. Indeed, if you didn't know the game, you would stand well back from the table. That's just common sense. Yet every day, thousands of people invest in the market on the basis of sketchy information, without knowing the pitfalls, or how the market works. These people are obviously playing with a handicap.

The reason I have written this book—which is aimed at anyone who invests or is thinking of investing—is to improve your odds for success. I say "odds" because all investments contain an element of risk, and hence are a gamble. The basic difference between throwing a pair of dice against the wall and buying a Government of Canada bond is the degree of risk. What a pair of dice and a government bond have in common is that you can lose your shirt on both of them. (It is, however, more respectable to drop a bundle on bonds than by shooting craps.)

When I came into the securities business in 1958, the choice of investments was limited to bonds, "straight" preferreds, common stocks, a few mutual funds, and commodities. Today, there are many sophisticated variations of these securities as well as a host of new products such as index futures, stock, bond and commodity options, precious metal warrants, and tax shelters.

Knowing what's out there—and how these securities can be employed to best advantage—is critical to your success. I can't tell you how to make a million dollars by next Tuesday, but I can explain the game and suggest strategies that will enhance your potential for profit.

In recalling experiences with clients—which are all true—I have used fictitious names to save these good people embarrassment, and me possible law suits. I should also add that the opinions in this book are entirely my own, and do not necessarily reflect the views or policies of the firm with which I am associated.

The Oxford Dictionary defines a *labyrinth* as being "a complicated irregular structure with many passages hard to find way through or about without guidance." This is also a fair description of the securities market. Having said that, I don't know of a better or a more exciting place to make money. After more than a quarter century of close contact with the market I still find it exhilarating, even though I've taken my lumps on more than one occasion. On the subject of losses, experience may be the best teacher but it is the most expensive way to learn.

My hope is that *The Money Labyrinth* will steer you clear of the hazards, and substantially improve your investment performance. If I can entertain you along the way, so much the better.

S.E.W.
Ottawa

THE MONEY LABYRINTH

CHAPTER 1

Why Put Your Money in the Market?

THE CHOICE OF investments ranges from the bland to the exotic. Investments in this sense means anything in which you choose to put your money—from a savings account to a collection of vintage comic books.

At the risk of stating the obvious, the purpose of investing is to get a return on your money. This return can be in the form of income or an increase in value—capital appreciation. A savings account is an income investment, while vintage comic books would only be bought for capital appreciation. A dividend paying stock is a good example of an investment that offers *both* income and capital appreciation. *The Money Labyrinth* is primarily concerned with stocks and similar securities, but before considering them let's take a look at some of the other investment alternatives.

The savings account is the most popular income investment in Canada. It is offered by banks, trust companies and other financial institutions under a variety of names, most of which include the words "savings" or "deposit." (Some also use "plus" or "bonus" as a grabber.) Basically, there are only two types of savings accounts: one which permits you to write cheques and one which does not. Most institutions offer both types of account. Interest is credited on the basis of your daily, monthly, or yearly *minimum* balance, depending on the terms. The minimum feature has to be watched, because if you make a large withdrawal it can dramatically reduce your return, even though you top up the account the next day. The minimum is there for a purpose—to discourage you from withdrawing your money. For the same reason, chequing accounts always pay a lower rate of interest than non-chequing accounts.

Here we stumble upon a basic principle of usury (or banking if you prefer) *the longer money is lent the more valuable it is to the borrower.* When you open a savings account you are in fact *lending* the institution your money, money which in turn is recycled out in loans to customers. Since the balances in non-chequing accounts are more stable than in chequing accounts, the institution pays more for this longer term money. It need hardly be mentioned that the institution charges a significantly higher rate on its loans than it pays on its deposits. The difference or "spread"—between the rate you receive on your deposit and what is charged on the loan—is the institution's profit.

As a digression, I feel sorry for people who allow themselves to be intimidated when asking for a loan. If you are a reasonable credit risk, you should remember that you are doing the bank a *favour* by giving it your business. Banks don't make money paying interest on deposits, they make it by charging interest on loans. Bankers don't like to be reminded of this fact, but nevertheless it is true.

The interest rate fluctuates on both types of savings accounts, but the non-chequing rate is always higher by a half to three quarters of one per cent. In relation to other income investments, the rate paid on savings accounts is normally at the lower end of the spectrum. The main advantages of a savings account are safety and liquidity. The main disadvantage is its low rate of return. During the past decade inflation has eaten away all or most of the interest paid on savings accounts. When you consider the tax bite as well, many depositors have actually had a *negative* return. I haven't had a savings account for years, but use a current account to pay my bills, and when there's a surplus I look for a short term note.

I can't leave the subject of savings accounts without mentioning the story of my wife's great aunt, who was known in the family as "Fat Aunt." This plump lady lived on the income from her father's estate, which was remitted to her monthly by the Royal Trust. Being mindful of the need to set something aside for a rainy day, she systematically deposited her excess income in a savings account with the Bank of Montreal. After Fat Aunt went to her Great Reward, her executors discovered she had accumulated more than one million dollars in this account. That was the good news. The bad news was that for all those years, it had only been earning between one and two per cent. The moral of this tale is that a savings account is a safe place to store your money, but a hell of a poor place to invest it.

Fat Aunt should have taken her hoard and invested it on a short term basis. Had she done so, she would have maintained the same liquidity, but earned a better return. All the banks and trust companies offer plans whereby you can invest sums of money from one day to one year. These investments are known by a variety of names such as "time deposits," "term notes," or "deposit receipts." For simplicity I will refer to them as time deposits.

Time deposits bear a higher rate of interest than savings accounts because your money is invested for a given term, specified in days, e.g., thirty days, with a prearranged maturity date. The old rule applies that the longer the term, the higher the rate of interest e.g., a ninety day deposit pays more than a thirty day deposit. Also, amounts over one hundred thousand dollars receive a higher or "premium" rate than lesser amounts for the same term. *In the money lending game, bigger is better.* The minimum amount needed to buy a time deposit is usually one thousand to five thousand dollars. If you want to withdraw your funds before the maturity date you may do so, but you will be penalized with a lower rate of interest. (This is a best case scenario; depending upon the circumstances and the issuer, you may forfeit *all* the interest.) As with savings accounts and other debt instruments, the rate of interest is always computed on an *annual basis*, which means that if you have one thousand dollars on deposit for one year at a rate of ten per cent you will receive one hundred dollars interest (10% of $1000), but if you have the same amount invested for thirty days, you will earn approximately

$12.50 or one twelfth of that amount. It is easy to arrange a time deposit, just go into your friendly bank or trust company and they will be happy to oblige.

When you decide to invest in a time deposit you will probably be encouraged to buy a longer term maturity. (Remember, the longer the term, the more valuable it is to the borrower.) My advice is to stick with thirty to ninety day maturities. You will pass up a quarter or a half of one per cent, but you will maintain liquidity—which is the purpose of a short term note. For convenience, you can arrange to have your time deposit "rolled over" automatically on the day it matures. This way there is no need to go into the bank and your money is continually at work. Your funds will be reinvested at the *current* rate (which may be higher or lower than the original one) but this unknown factor can be an advantage. Should interest rates soar, as they have done several times in recent years, you will profit from the higher rates.

When interest is earned on interest, as it does when you roll over a deposit, money compounds with surprising speed. For example, a sum compounded at eight per cent doubles in nine years. This might suggest that rolling over a large amount of money for an extended period would be a clever and risk free way to invest. The drawback to this strategy is that interest is fully taxable, and the *net* after tax return you receive will almost certainly be less than the rate of inflation. Once again, you will be faced with an erosion of capital.

Banks and other lending institutions also offer Guaranteed Investment Certificates, which have a term of from one to five years. The trust and loan companies flog these with great gusto because it is a marvellous way to lock in money to loan out for mortgages. I use the term "lock" with good reason. A condition of most guaranteed investment certificates is that you are committed for the full term. The only way you can get your money out before maturity is to die—an option with limited appeal. If you are really in a bind for funds, some issuers will *lend* your money back to you (at a higher rate than you lent it to them), but the contract still remains in force.

I remember a few years ago when Canada Savings Bonds were offered at 19½%, that some of my clients were unable to take advantage of the issue because they were shackled with guaranteed investment certificates paying half that rate. Canada Savings Bonds would have given them better security, more interest, and complete liquidity—but there was nothing they could do. If you are determined to buy a guaranteed investment certificate, it pays to shop around. Rates vary slightly among the major institutions, and by shopping you can get the best rate on whatever maturity you have in mind. *The Globe and Mail* publishes a summary of current rates each week, which will save you time. The only word of warning I would give is to restrict your search to the *largest and strongest* institutions. Do *not* be lured by an extra half point into putting your money with one of the fringe or lesser companies. The reason they pay more is because their credit rating is not as high as the big institutions. This brings up another investment maxim: *the lower the credit rating, the higher the cost to borrow.* If you are putting money on deposit your first requirement is safety—so it is senseless to risk your entire investment for a fractionally higher return. The frightened depositors who lined up outside the offices of Seaway Trust and Crown Trust after the Rosenberg Affair became public, would agree with this statement.

Actually, most banks, trust companies, and mortgage loan companies are members of the Canada Deposit Insurance Corporation. This Crown Corporation insures deposits (including notes up to five years) against loss because of the insolvency of a member institution. The limit of coverage for each depositor with any one institution is sixty thousand dollars. This means that if you have a fifty thousand dollar deposit or guaranteed investment certificate you are completely covered should the institution go belly up. If you have one hundred thousand dollars in a certificate, forty thousand is *not* covered by the Canada Deposit Insurance Corporation. Because the limit applies to the institution, you can't increase your coverage by having accounts with several branch offices, the only way you can do this is by having accounts with *different institutions*.

The advantages of a guaranteed investment certificate are that it is safe, it pays a reasonable rate of interest, and the rate is fixed for the term of the note. The disadvantages are that there can be no liquidity—you can be locked in—the interest is fully taxable, and there is no opportunity for capital appreciation. On balance, except for certain circumstances, it is a poor investment.

Personal mortgages are another form of term investment. Personal mortgages are loans secured by real estate, such as a house, farm, or land. The term is usually five or ten years and the rate varies with the risk. The safest type of mortgage is a First Mortgage, which has first call on the proceeds from the sale of the real estate in the event of a default by the borrower. A Second Mortgage is more risky, because it gets nothing until the first mortgage has been paid in full. A Third Mortgage ranks behind a second mortgage, and should be bought with the fingers crossed. Personal mortgages are sold to investors by mortgage brokers and some lawyers. (Lawyers find mortgages a profitable sideline because they make a fee from both the lender and the borrower—in this type of transaction a lawyer can wield his ball-point pen with the efficiency of a revolver.) Even though there may be ample assets covering a mortgage, the interest rate will normally be higher than a guaranteed investment certificate.

A mortgage should pay a higher rate—it's an even worse investment. Some people think that because a mortgage is secured by real estate it's a safe haven in bad times. The truth is that when the economy turns down, real estate prices fall with it. During the Great Depression thousands of mortgage holders were wiped out. Nor is a mortgage an inflation hedge—when a mortgage matures, you get devalued dollars out the other end. The rate of interest paid in the interim is fully taxable, so you really get a low true rate of return. Liquidity is another problem (try hawking a personal mortgage). If you do find a buyer, you will be forced to sell at a hefty discount.

I can only think of two reasons for owning a personal mortgage. One would be to facilitate the sale of your house by taking back a mortgage from the buyer. The other would be to facilitate the purchase of a separate dwelling for your mother-in-law.

Real estate can be a rewarding investment if you are an *owner* rather than a *lender*. By this I mean purchasing a house, some land or an apartment building with the object of selling it at a higher price for a capital gain. It is done every day, and many people make a lot of money out of real estate. The game, however, entails an element of risk. What heightens the risk, is that the secret to making big profits in real estate is to use leverage—or put more simply, other people's money. Thus when you buy a property you try and borrow as much of the purchase price as possible, and put as little of your own money into it as you can. This works beautifully if the value of your property rises—you get a much bigger bang for your buck—but if it falls, you are on the hook in short order.

Real estate is really a game for the experts, but when a boom gets under way hordes of novices are attracted by the action. Inevitably, many get hurt—the collapse of housing prices in 1981 and 1982 devastated speculators across the country, particularly in cities like Calgary and Vancouver. The big guys were also caught in the downdraft, but most have survived to play another day.

My own experience in real estate has been very profitable. But I am not an expert, and I learned this the hard way. About ten years ago I had a client who was an extremely successful real estate entrepreneur. We had done business together for some time, and I thought he was a pretty good fellow. One day he invited me into a syndicate that was going to build a large apartment building. With his track record, I thought I couldn't lose. I put in around twenty thousand dollars for my tiny slice of the pie, and made additional payments to him in the ensuing months. Eventually, I got twitchy about my investment—the project seemed to be stalled—and started to ask questions, but got no satisfactory answers. I then asked him if he wanted to buy me out, and he agreed to buy my interest for the price I had paid for it. A few weeks after this transaction I was stopped on the street by a friend in the real estate business who told me that I had been cheated by my former partner. What had happened was that before he bought my interest, he had already made a deal to sell the entire project for a fat profit. I got my share, but it took me three years of litigation and we ended up in court.

What I don't like about real estate is its lack of liquidity, except at distress prices. There are other drawbacks, such as rent controls on income properties, and legislation that prohibits the purchase of farmland for speculation. I don't quibble with these laws—they are undoubtedly a good thing—but they certainly lessen the appeal of real estate as an investment. For the average person I think the best real estate investment is to own your own house or apartment. I would also make it a priority to pay off the mortgage. This may sound like old fashioned and ultra-conservative advice, but it was only a few years ago that mortgages were being renewed at twenty per cent. I wouldn't be surprised to see rates go to that level again. And I would add that until you have a substantial equity in your home—say at least fifty per cent—you shouldn't invest in anything else, including the stock market.

Many people invest in collectables—works of art, stamps, books, vintage cars, coins, firearms, cigar bands or whatever. The list is almost endless. None of these yield any income, and all are bought for capital appreciation.

In a small way I have bought prints, paintings, and books as an investment. At least that's how I rationalize their purchase. When I browse through catalogues I am gratified to see that my acquisitions have all gone up in value, or most have. But who am I kidding? If I bought a print nine years ago and it has doubled, it has not even kept pace with inflation. (Remember, money compounded at eight per cent doubles in nine years.) The other catch is that I bought these *retail* but if I want to sell them I will have to sell at the *wholesale* price—so the item offered in the catalogue at two hundred dollars would only fetch half that amount, or one hundred dollars if bought by the dealer. Some years ago I actually went through this exercise, and I realized fifty cents on the dollar for a dozen limited editions.

The people who make money in collectables are the professionals, not the amateurs. For the average person, buying collectables is a hobby. Our payoff comes from the pleasure of owning the items, not from selling them.

Life insurance is another popular investment. I am all for life insurance as a form of protection, and maintain substantial coverage myself. But a word of caution, the boys in the life insurance industry are masters at the shell game, and keep the pea moving with the speed of light.

After you cut away all the frills there are only two basic types of life insurance. One is "term" and the other is "whole" life. (Variations and combinations of these two come in a bewildering array, and there are new hybrids appearing every day.) Term insurance is like the coverage on your house. You pay for term insurance year after year, and when you stop paying, that's it. There is no residual value. If you die while term insurance is in force the policy pays its full face value. Which seems perfectly reasonable. Whole life is similar to term *except* that as the years go by you build up a residual or cash value in the policy. If you outlive the policy, you receive a sum of money, but if you die while it's in force, you simply get the face value of the policy. The premium cost of term insurance is a fraction that of whole life. The difference in the premiums is due to the fact that you build up a cash value in whole life. The commission paid on term is also a fraction that paid on whole life. The reason for this difference is that whole life is far more profitable to the insurance companies and they want to encourage their salespeople to sell it.

The big commission is why insurance salespeople push whole life. In most cases, particularly with heads of young families, it is a grave disservice to recommend whole life. Consider the position of a father with three young children. If he can only afford two hundred dollars a year for insurance, is it better for him to buy one hundred thousand dollars of term or should he buy twenty thousand dollars of whole life? If he gets run over by a truck will his widow be happier to get one hundred thousand dollars or twenty thousand dollars? Will she care whether it was term or whole life?

The insurance industry justifies whole life on the basis that it forces people to save, and that it is an excellent investment. For a given premium it does force the holder to save—at the expense of coverage. As to whole life being a good investment, past results indicate that policies rarely keep up with inflation. If a person is unable to save, he would be far better to buy term insurance and to invest the surplus each year in one of the better mutual funds.

To sum up, everyone should have adequate insurance. Term insurance provides the cheapest protection, and is the best way to create an instant estate. Whole life insurance—under whatever name—should be avoided. The only way to invest in insurance is to buy the common shares of one of the insurance companies.

This brings us to the end of our tour of investments outside the securities markets. Each has its advantages and its disadvantages. I like to make money as much as the next person, and have tried many outside investments. Now I stay with the securities markets—they have variety, liquidity, and action. To learn more about them, read on.

CHAPTER 2

Choosing a Broker

My BROTHER JOHN can usually count on a laugh—at my expense—when he describes a stockbroker as being a "leech on the side of industry." Disgruntled investors have also been known to refer to their broker as a "tout," a "shill," or a "thief." In my experience, most brokers are honest, and they try their best to make money for their clients. But some brokers are better at the game than others. In fact, brokers are no different than any other type of businessman—there are good ones and there are bad ones. To choose a good broker you should know something about the securities industry, and the stock exchanges in Canada.

Toronto is Canada's financial centre, with Montreal and Vancouver having lesser spheres of influence. It wasn't always this way. When I came into the business in 1958, Montreal was the headquarters of many important financial institutions. Today, most of these institutions, as well as the major old-line Montreal investment houses—such as Dominion Securities, Pitfield, and Nesbitt Thomson—have shifted their main operations to Toronto. Montreal is still designated as the head office of some of these companies, but Toronto is where the decisions are made.

The same situation exists with regard to the stock exchanges. In 1983, more than six billion shares worth nearly forty billion dollars were traded on Canadian stock exchanges. The Toronto Stock Exchange accounted for more than seventy-five per cent, or thirty billion dollars of the total value. The Montreal Exchange (which is the oldest) trailed far behind with approximately five billion dollars worth of transactions. It should, however, be noted that the Montreal Exchange is making an aggressive comeback by introducing innovative measures. The Vancouver Stock Exchange had a trading value of less than four billion, but traded more shares than all the other exchanges combined. In 1983 the average value of a share traded on the Vancouver exchange was less than one dollar, and most were mining or oil stocks—which is why the Vancouver Stock Exchange has been nicknamed "Vegas North" and "The World's Largest Casino." The Alberta Stock Exchange, which is located in Calgary, and the Winnipeg Stock Exchange accounted for a negligible percentage of the total volume.

Before looking at the securities industry, I will try to clear up the confusion that surrounds the names that the companies operate under. Some are called "investment dealers" or "securities dealers," others are called "stockbrokers" or "brokerage firms." The historic difference between an investment dealer and a stockbroker is that an investment dealer acts as *principal* while the stockbroker acts as *agent*. Thus when you make a trade with an investment dealer, he either sells the security to you from his inventory, or buys it from you for his own account. The difference between the buying and selling price is his profit on the transaction. A stockbroker, on the other hand, does not *own* the security at any time, he acts as your agent and the profit he makes comes from the commission he charges on the transaction.

Investment dealers are also "underwriters" of new issues. When governments, municipalities, or corporations want to raise money by the sale of bonds or shares, an investment dealer (or a group of investment dealers) will underwrite the issue. This means that the dealer will buy the entire amount for a fixed price. Having bought the issue, the dealer will then mark up the price (the mark up is his profit) and sell it to the public. After the issue is sold, the dealer is obliged to maintain an ongoing market. If the dealer is unable to sell all the issue, or if he is forced to reduce its price, he bears the loss—not the government or corporation. For this reason, underwriting entails some risk, but it can be highly lucrative. Underwriting is also important to the economy because it provides capital for those who need it.

Today, there are approximately one hundred firms in the securities business in Canada. They vary in size from one man operations to companies with over one thousand employees. Many of these firms, particularly the larger ones, are *both* investment dealers and stockbrokers. (To further complicate the picture, some brokers will act as principals when amassing large blocks of stock for resale to institutional clients—but this is of academic interest.) The most influential force in the industry is the Investment Dealers Association of Canada.

The Investment Dealers Association was founded in 1916 at the request of the Canadian government. It is the national self-regulatory body for the securities industry. It works in conjunction with the stock exchanges and the provincial securities commissions. Its purpose—aside from the welfare of its members —is to enforce high standards of conduct and to protect the public. To this end, there is a National Contingency Fund which was set up with the exchanges to reimburse clients if a member firm should go bankrupt. The Association also continually monitors the conduct and the financial positions of its members. The Investment Dealers Association maintains close links with the securities commissions and is responsible for most of the educational courses within the industry. For these reasons, I would confine your search for a broker to members of the Investment Dealers Association. This shouldn't prove too restrictive, as there are roughly seventy member firms with more than five hundred offices. These firms handle more than ninety per cent of the investment business in Canada.

The Investment Dealers Association of Canada should *not* be confused with the Broker-Dealers' Association of Ontario, which is a group of approximately eight firms in the Toronto area. At this writing, none of the members of the Broker-Dealers' Association belong to a Canadian stock exchange, and all deal in unlisted junior resource stocks.

The mention of speculative mining and oil stocks brings up another word of warning. If you ever get a long distance call from a broker who wants you to buy a "penny dreadful" say "no." The standard sales pitch—which is delivered in an excited voice—goes something like this: An adventurous little company has just discovered a fantastic mine. (You may substitute "oil well" for "mine" if you wish.) The drilling results, which are incredible, have not been released yet. As soon as the results are made public, the price of the shares will soar. Fortunately for you, it is not too late. By a stroke of luck, the broker has one thousand shares that are still available at the original underwriting price of seventy cents. He will let you have these shares, providing you mail a certified cheque or money order to him immediately. It is a chance of a lifetime, because the stock will soon be worth eight or ten dollars.

The first thing you should ask yourself when you get this sort of call is, "if it is such a sure thing, why is a total stranger taking the trouble and expense to tell me?" (It is unlikely that the Good Fairy whispered your name in his ear.) The answer, of course, is that you are on a sucker list. And you are not the only one. I often get inquiries from people who have bought these stocks. When they ask me what they should do, I tell them to sell their shares. I can't remember anyone who ever got his original investment back. If you really must gamble on a long shot, you would be better off to go to the racetrack. You will probably lose your money, but at least you will have the satisfaction of seeing the horses run.

Getting back to the choice of a broker—as I mentioned, I would rule out those firms that are not members of the Investment Dealers Association. This is the first step in the process of elimination. The next step is to decide whether you want to deal with a large or a small firm.

Small firms usually operate from a single location with a small staff. Those that cater to a certain type of clientele—such as institutional investors—are known in the industry as "boutiques." Some small firms provide excellent service. The main advantage of being a client of a small investment house is that you may have personal contact with the proprietor—in fact he may look after your account. If it is a good sized account, you will be treated royally. The disadvantages of small firms are that they often have limited research facilities, limited access to underwritings, and few seats on exchanges. These disadvantages mean that you, the client, will be restricted in your investment scope.

Large firms also have advantages and disadvantages. By large I mean firms that are both stock brokers and underwriters, with a dozen or more branches. These firms are known in the industry as "integrated" houses. An integrated firm is like a general store—with commodity, underwriting, and money market departments as well as bond trading and stockbroking facilities. Large firms spend heavily on research, they participate in many new issues, and they have seats on numerous exchanges. What does this mean to the client? It means convenience, in the form of one stop shopping, and it means access to a variety of investment opportunities.

Research is critical to good investment decisions. If the firm you deal with publishes sound and timely information, you are well on your way to making money. Underwritings permit you to buy new issues at the original offering price, *without* paying a commission. Often a new issue can be resold for an immediate profit. When you buy or sell stocks, the efficiency of the transaction is influenced by whether the firm is a member of the exchange on which the shares are listed. If the firm does not have a seat on the exchange, it must engage another broker to execute the trade. This can result in slow and sloppy service on your orders. If, however, you deal with a firm that is a member of many exchanges, you can expect fast and efficient executions.

I would suggest that on balance, an investor should choose one of the large integrated houses. But there are hazards that you should be aware of. The quality of research varies widely within the industry, and it varies from analyst to analyst *within each firm*. This happens because some people are smarter than others. A more sinister factor is *biased research* due to an underwriting connection. If an investment house regularly underwrites the securities of a company, it is not likely to publish a negative report on that company. Usually this is a sin of ommission, but there have been instances where an underwriter has "primed the pump" with a glowing research report just prior to selling a lousy issue to the public. (This is standard procedure with the fringe operators, but it occasionally happens in large firms.)

Underwriting is big business—in 1983 more than six billion dollars worth of Canadian preferred and common shares were underwritten. New issues can be tricky to judge. They are not always a boon to own—sometimes they go *down* in price after they have been sold to investors. For this reason, the purchase of a new issue must be made as carefully as any other security transaction.

A good way to select an investment house is to ask friends or acquaintances who are involved in the market. Eventually the names of several firms—or at least one—will emerge as having the best reputation. Having narrowed your choice to not more than three houses, your next step is to phone the manager of the local branches of these firms. The purpose of your call is to arrange an appointment to see one of his brokers. (If the name of a broker in a firm has been recommended to you, phone directly to that person.) When you speak to a manager, it is not necessary to tell him that you are shopping, but you should give him a clear idea of your investment objectives and the potential size of your account. This information will permit the manager to match you off with a broker who can best serve your needs. (That is the *theory*, but he may just pass you on to most junior salesman, the one who is scrambling to build a clientele.) Now comes the most critical part of your search, and the one that requires sound judgement on your part—the interview with the broker.

I have used the terms "broker" and "salesman" interchangeably, as they are one and the same. Other common names are "registered representative," "account executive," and "customers' man." (The latter designation is now obsolete, because there are women brokers, and the term "customers' woman" or "customers' person" would be ludicrous.) The most correct designation is "registered representative" because everyone who deals in securities must be registered with a provincial securities commission. Before obtaining a licence to deal in securities the person must also pass an exam, and have at least three months experience in the business. The term "account executive" was imported from the United States, and was lifted from the advertising industry. I have only known one person who had the gall to call himself an account executive. This ambitious young chap began his career with Royal Securities on the same day that I did. As we were both trainees we shared a desk in the outer office. I used to hear him on the phone introducing himself in a squeaky voice to prospective clients with these words:

"Good afternoon Mrs. Bloggs, this is Mister J. Murgatroyd Bloodhound, I am an account executive with Royal Securities." Murgatroyd worked hard, and he prospered as an account executive. Unfortunately, when he eventually became a real executive, and head of another firm, his fortunes went into a precipitous decline. The moral of this story is to be leery of anyone who calls himself an account executive. He may be a competent broker, but he may also suffer from an ego problem. The most popular name—and the one that I shall use—is broker. Broker has no sexist connotation, and it describes the registered representative's main function. Although the investment business has traditionally been a male domain, today between five and ten per cent of the brokers in Canada are women. (There are also some first rate securities analysts in the industry who are women.) Thus, if you have a preference, you can choose either a man or a woman to be your broker.

It will also help you to know that brokers are by nature highly independent. Although they are employees of the firms with whom they are associated, most brokers are not paid a salary but earn their living from commissions. These commissions are generated from the business they do with their own clientele. Brokers' earnings fluctuate with the swings in the market—when the market is active they make lots of money, but when the market is in the doldrums they starve. Because a broker's clientele represents his earning power, he guards it jealously and is usually on the lookout for new accounts. (He needs to keep replenishing his clientele to offset the attrition which takes place for a variety of reasons, particularly death and disenchantment.) A good broker's first loyalty is to his clients, his second is to his firm. It is also true that most investors have a loyalty to an *individual* rather than to a firm. I have proved this to my own satisfaction twice, when I moved from one firm to another and was able to take the majority of my clientele with me. This is not unusual, and happens in the business every day. However, it does highlight another point—you will be dealing with a firm, but for all practical purposes that firm will be represented by a *single person*, your broker. This is why the choice of a broker is so important to you.

To make this choice intelligently, a face to face meeting is essential. If you rely on a telephone interview, you are only using your sense of hearing to size up a person who can make—or lose—a lot of money for you. By going into his office and sitting down with him you can not only see whether he has close-set shifty eyes, but you can also check the facilities of the office. (In this connection, forget the decor, but try to assess whether the place is run efficiently.) It is also well to remember that while you are interviewing the broker, and dangling your bag of gold before his eyes, he will be interviewing you.

To save time, you should be frank with each other. You need not fear that the information you divulge will be repeated, for brokers treat all business dealings as confidential. This is not surprising, as money is an exceedingly sensitive subject. Most people would rather discuss their marital situation than reveal their bank balance. Indeed, I had a married couple as clients who each made me promise not to let the other spouse know of their dealings—and two brothers who insisted on the same arrangement. (The couple are now divorced, but the brothers are still together.) So you can speak freely.

One of the most unnerving interviews I ever had was with a man who was a psychic. His name was Cyril, and he was referred to me by another client. Cyril had accomplished some quite extraordinary psychic feats, and he unquestionably possessed the gift of second sight. The prospect of meeting him made me uneasy, but this was offset by the intriguing potential of having him as a client. When he swept into my office I was struck by his energy—he almost radiated sparks. During our interview he fixed me with a glittering stare, and I was sure that he was reading my innermost thoughts. This made me uncomfortable, because I was thinking that with Cyril forecasting market moves, I could make a hell of a lot of money. Unfortunately, it didn't work out that way. Cyril opened a margin account, and with supreme confidence proceeded to pick a succession of losers. Eventually his psychic powers waned to such a degree that he was unable to recognize margin calls, even when they were sent to him by telegram. Our business relationship, which had held such promise, ended on a sour note.

What you want to learn from your interview with the broker is whether he is competent, whether he understands your investment objectives, and whether he wants to look after your account.

Investing is more an art than a science. For this reason compe-. tence is *not* related to the number of degrees a broker may have picked up in university. What a good broker must have is a "feel" for the market and training in all facets of the business, including options and commodities. Nor are the social graces a criterion for excellence. One of the best brokers I know is a country boy, who makes grammatical errors, but who can consistently spot investment opportunities. His talent lies in his feel for the market. Some people have it, but the majority lack this gift. Length of service is another way to measure competence, because in the investment game there is no substitute for experience. You can find out how long a broker has been in the business by casually asking how long he has been with the firm. You may be surprised to learn that the grey haired gentleman opposite you has only been in the business six months, having retired from the army after thirty-five years as a cook—or he may have been a broker for a quarter of a century. Novice brokers are enthusiastic, but they tend to be naive about their firm's research and underwritings. You want someone with enough experience to screen recommendations and new issues for you. Some novice brokers are shrewd, but most are like young robins, inclined to swallow anything that is fed to them. This can be costly for their clients.

Before the broker can understand your investment objectives, you must know them yourself. This may sound like a stupid statement, but it is surprising how many people are unsure of what they want from their portfolio. If you don't have an investment goal in mind—be it capital gain, income, or a combination of both—your results will suffer. Less than a month ago I had a career woman in my office who had a large sum of money to invest, but she had no idea what she wanted from her portfolio. Although a successful and intelligent person, she hadn't given the question any thought. When I pressed her for an answer, she became quite flustered. The problem was solved by going over her priorities, and through a process of elimination we worked out her investment objective. One of the things that I suggested to her was that she consult her accountant to confirm that her tax position was as she described it to me. Tax is a major consideration in any investment strategy, and the place to get tax advice is from an accountant, *not* from a broker.

Be quite sure that when you tell the broker your investment objective, you mean what you say. At the height of the last bull market—when euphoria was in the air and junior stocks were soaring—a schoolteacher named Alex came to me and said that he wanted to speculate in the high fliers. I pointed out to him that this was an extremely dangerous game. Alex said that he knew it was risky, but he had twenty thousand dollars which he was prepared to lose, and that if he lost the entire amount it would not affect his standard of living. I chose some stocks for him, and he chose some, and initially things went well. But a few months later the market took the gas, and Alex lost most of his money. It then turned out that he had not expected to suffer a heavy loss, and he was very bitter about it. The whole sad episode could have been avoided if he had told me at the outset that he was *really* only prepared to lose a modest amount. I should add that I lost Alex as a client—and I don't expect any referrals from him.

My mistake with Alex—aside from disastrous market timing— was to assume that he was a genuine gambler. There are clients, and I have several, who love to gamble. These people know the odds, and accept their losses philosophically. What they want is *action*, and to this end they will play any type of game to get it. When the securities markets are dormant, they hop on a jet and fly to Atlantic City or Las Vegas. At the casinos, there is action to be found at any time of the year. As soon as stocks become active again, they return to the market. Because these high rollers trade frequently and generate huge commissions, they are greeted with joy by their brokers.

The mention of gamblers—and losses—brings up another factor to consider when setting your investment objective. Is your investment goal compatible with your temperament? For example, if capital gain is your first priority, this would suggest a portfolio with a fair percentage of "growth" stocks. By their nature, growth stocks are volatile and tend to fluctuate widely in price. Would this type of investment make you nervous? If the answer is yes, then you should reconsider your strategy. It is not worth the candle to hold common stocks (even good ones) if it increases your level of anxiety. You would be better off to buy a growth type mutual fund, or to pay an investment advisor to manage your portfolio. I have a friend named Sue who is temperamentally unsuited to play the market, but she insists on doing so. She never makes much, because as soon as one of her stocks hits the slightest turbulence, she sells it. I have told Sue several times that she should stick to the bond market (where the swings are less dramatic) and forget about common stocks. So far she has ignored my advice, although she does dabble in bonds from time to time. Sue is one of those people who is both fascinated and terrified by the stock market. She reminds me of a child who stands bravely at the edge of the water until a wave comes in, and then flees up the beach. Sue, unless she undergoes a frontal lobotomy, will never be comfortable owning common stocks.

When you outline your financial position and investment objective to the broker, he will listen attentively, and probably make notes. He does this because a cardinal rule in the business is to know the client. Assuming that he fully understands your objective, you must also try to determine whether he is genuinely interested in being of service. Whether he *cares*, and is prepared to make an *ongoing commitment* to your investment program. Some brokers are "stock jockeys" who latch on to a high flier and sell it indiscriminately to all their clients. This is alright if you are a speculator, but if you are an investor you need someone with a portfolio approach who will consider whether a security fits into your overall program. Your broker should maintain an up-to-date list of your securities and keep you informed of any changes that affect them. In addition to suggesting switches in your holdings, he should only offer you new issues that compliment your portfolio. When the inevitable administrative errors occur, it is your broker's responsibility to sort things out. A good broker not only enters your orders, but he should phone you *promptly* to advise you when they have been filled. It is aggravating, and sometimes nervewracking, to have an order in to buy or sell a security and not know whether it has been executed. If a broker is casual about reporting back to you he is either slothful or indifferent—or both. Finally, you should be able to phone your broker at any time if you need advice, without feeling compelled to place an order to justify the call. But when you phone, remember that the broker has other clients, and don't waste his time with idle chat.

During the interview the broker will be weighing you as a potential client. The first thing that he will want to establish is the size of your account. Some successful brokers simply do not have the time to deal with small accounts. This may seem harsh, but it is a fact of life. The broker will also want to know what your previous experience has been with other investment houses. If you have been dissatisfied with several *reputable* firms, this will flash a warning signal to him that you may be a chronic malcontent. Experience has taught me to avoid this type of investor—they are never satisfied. Another question is whether the prospective client already has a broker—and whether he will be competing against the other broker for the client's business. I don't like this type of situation because the conflicting recom- mendations of the other broker usually make a hash of my attempts to structure a portfolio. Unless it is a large and sophisti- cated account, I ask the client to make a choice between us. The advantage of having more than one broker is that you get research and new issues from several sources. The disadvantage is that unless you are an *active trader*, with a very big portfolio, you will be an insignificant account with all your brokers. You will get much better service if you are a good account with one.

What is the definition of a small account? If you asked a dozen brokers, you'd probably get a dozen different answers. It can't be quantified by the value of the client's portfolio, because it is the *commissions* that count. Another factor is the average size of each commission. I have a client whose holdings consist of short term Canada bonds worth half a million dollars. From a broker's point of view, he is a small account because these bonds gener- ate little commission. I can think of another client with a portfolio one fifth that size, who is an aggressive stock trader. His commis- sions are quite substantial. If I was forced to pick a number, I would say that clients who generate less than two thousand dollars *per year* in commissions, are small accounts. I don't look for small accounts, but some of my favourite clients fall into this category.

The foundation of a solid relationship between a client and a broker is mutual trust. If either party has the slightest doubt about the other's integrity, you shouldn't do business with each other. One reason for this is that there are no written contracts (except for margin and special trading agreements) *before* a transaction takes place. Orders to buy and sell are all given *verbally*, usually over the phone. If a broker deliberately misleads a client it is very difficult to prove. If a client backs out of an order, the broker personally bears the loss. Once you have chosen a broker, you should accept his advice in good faith. Or as Bert, one of the rougher diamonds in my clientele, said to me:

"Mr. Woods, if you screw up too often, you don't get no more of my business. Until then, we run!"

Bert and I are still running. I enjoy dealing with Bert because he trusts me, and I know exactly where I stand with him. He is also a good loser, and he gives credit when credit is due. This is unusual, as many clients like to take the credit for their winners, but when they lose, they blame it on their broker.

If you choose to deal with a discount house—be it a bank or a broker—you won't be able to blame anyone but yourself. Discount brokers execute stock transactions at a much lower rate of commission than the full service houses. They may be compared to a self-serve gas bar, in that you get the product at a saving but no service. Discount brokers do not provide advice, they simply take orders. If you rely on your own research, and have no interest in new issues, a discount broker might be worthwhile. I am biased on the subject because I work for a full service house, and wouldn't have it any other way. For the *average* investor, I think the benefits of a full service house far outweigh the savings obtained from a discount broker. Some of these benefits are hard to measure, like being able to discuss a security with your broker when you're worried about it, or being able to ask his advice when you're contemplating a trade. Then again, if you're the sort who will drive out of your way to fill up at a self-serve gas bar, and you enjoy changing your own spark plugs, maybe a discount broker is for you.

Speaking of commissions, and discounts, it should be added that commissions vary among the full service houses, and are subject to discounting. Since negotiated rates came into force in April 1983, there has been a considerable amount of jockeying in the industry to provide the most competitive rates. This factor, competition, has ensured that no full service house has gotten far out of line with the others. Commission rates are whatever the traffic will bear, and frequently change. The one thing that you can be sure of is *the larger the order, the lower the commission per share*. This means that if the commission per share is forty cents on an order of one hundred shares, it might be twenty cents on an order of one thousand shares. As with anything else, it pays to shop in bulk.

The other day one of my clients chided me for the commissions that brokers charge, and all the money they make. He was in a jovial mood because he had just made a nice turn in the market, and to show that there were no hard feelings on the subject, he told me the following story. It is a very old one, but you may not have heard it before.

The setting is the yacht basin at the foot of Wall Street, in New York. Two men are standing on the pier; one is a native New Yorker, the other is from the boonies. The New Yorker proudly points to the glistening yachts at anchor, and with a sweep of his hand says:

"Those are the brokers' yachts."

The yokel gazes at them in awe for several minutes, and then turning to his friend asks:

"Where are the customers' yachts?"

CHAPTER 3

Rules of the Game

THIS CHAPTER MAY sound tedious, but I would suggest you read it. To avoid boring you with a lot of unnecessary details I will stick to information you should know, and which will be useful when you invest. The rules are constantly changing, so even if you consider yourself an old pro at the game, you will probably learn something of value.

If you are a novice investor, the first thing you should know is how you open an account with a broker. It is quite simple, and can even be done over the telephone. All that is required is for the broker to fill out a New Client Application form. This form is mandatory throughout the industry, and must be completed by the broker—and accepted by his firm—before you can make a transaction.

The information you provide will be treated as confidential. The first questions are your name, address, telephone number(s) and Social Insurance Number. If you don't want to give your Social Insurance Number, you are not compelled to do so. The type of account you want, be it *cash* (payment in full for all trades) or *margin* (where the broker lends you money to finance your transactions), is recorded—you can have both if you wish. Assuming it is a cash account, the broker will need to know whether you want his firm to hold the securities, or if you want the certificates registered and sent to you. If it is a margin account, you will have to sign a Margin Agreement, and the securities will be held as collateral by the broker until paid in full. Any special instructions for the mailing of confirmations (invoices) or other special instructions, such as delivery of certificates to your bank, will be noted. In this connection, if you want to open a *joint account*, a supplementary form is required which must be signed by you and your partner. The broker will supply this form. In certain cases, a Guarantee may be required for an account. Here again, the broker has a standard form. If the account is a *personal holding company* or a *corporation*, a signed and sealed copy of the Corporate Resolution must be given to the broker.

Often, one person will enter orders on behalf of another person—such as a husband for his wife. This is perfectly legal *providing* a Trading Authorization is on file. This document states that the owner of the account authorizes a specific individual to execute trades on his or her behalf. Recently, a woman at a cocktail party told me that her husband, unknown to her, had instructed her broker to sell her holding in Mitel and to buy another company. Mitel stock subsequently went up tenfold while her shares in the other company went down. This happened some years ago, but she was still mad as a wet hen. I asked her if she had signed a Trading Authorization in favour of her husband. She had not, thus both her husband *and* her broker were at fault. I gather she chastized her husband, but if she had wished, she could also have taken legal action against the broker. That is why a Trading Authorization is essential if one person is going to enter orders for another.

Other questions on the New Client Application form concern your business and occupation. If you are a senior officer or a director of a company listed on an exchange or whose shares are traded over the counter, this must be recorded. The reason for this question is to find out if you are an *"insider"* and thus subject to certain restrictions and reporting procedures. Very few people are insiders. Your marital status is also of interest. If you're married, your spouse's name and occupation must be noted on the form. The broker, for his part, has to state whether he has met you and how long he has known you, and whether you were referred by another client. He must also declare if he has a direct or indirect interest in your account (this can happen with a spouse, a relative, or a business partner). If the broker has an interest, all the orders will be marked "PRO" (for "professional") and they will be subject to the Preferential Trading Rule. This rule ensures that when a regular client places an order to buy or sell a security at the *same* price as a "PRO" order, the regular client's order takes precedence.

Among the more personal questions are those concerning your age, your approximate net worth (which is arrived at by valuing your assets and deducting your debts) and your earnings per year. Net worth need not be precise, but your earnings should be accurate to within a few thousand dollars. You will also be asked where you bank, and the name of a person at that bank to whom the broker can refer. This is the normal extent of the check on your credit. I confess that I rarely phone the bank about a new client, but I do ask some searching questions before opening the account. So far—touch wood—I have never been stuck with a bad cheque.

The last section of the form is extremely important, because it deals with your investment objectives and your knowledge of the market. Your investment objectives are categorized as to "income," "long term growth," "speculation," etc., and each is given a percentage figure. For example, your investment objectives might be "50% income and 50% long term growth." Your knowledge of the market is graded as either "excellent," "good," "fair," or "nil." This part of the questionnaire is designed to *protect* you, and to ensure that the recommendations of the broker are suitable for your investment needs. If a widow, whose investment objectives were safety and income, lost money on a raft of speculative securities, the New Client Application form would provide evidence against the broker. (Curiously enough, there was a case in Toronto where an elderly grandmother tried to sue a broker for just that, but the New Client Application form showed clearly that she was a "shooter," and that she was only interested in speculative situations.)

The New Client Application form ties in with the cardinal rule of the investment industry, which is "know your client." This rule is drummed into brokers from the first day they enter the business. Knowing the client serves two main purposes: to ensure that investment recommendations are appropriate for the account, and to protect the broker. You may wonder why the broker needs protection. Aside from the financial risk, there are other hazards. Last Christmas, a clipping from *The Wall Street Journal* was placed on the notice board in our office. The headline of this story read "Disgruntled Investor Kidnaps, Beats Broker." Beside this bizarre headline some wag had scrawled in pen "Know Your Client!"

There is no need for you to sign the New Client Application form. When it is completed, it is signed by your broker and a partner or a director of the firm. Once this is done you are ready to place your first order.

For those who have never invested before, it might be useful to go through what happens when you place an order. Let us assume that you want to buy two hundred shares of Bell Enterprises Limited. You phone your broker and ask him what the "market" is on Bell common shares. He can give you the answer in the blink of an eye, because he has (or should have) a video terminal beside him. By punching certain letters on the keyboard, he has access to a variety of stock exchanges and can also retrieve a host of other financial data. Your broker enters the symbol for Bell, and reads you the information from the screen. What you want to know is the "bid" and the "ask" on the stock, and the last price at which it traded.

The "bid" is the price someone is willing to *buy* a "board lot" of shares, and the "ask" is the price someone is willing to *sell* a board lot. A board lot is a standard trading unit, in this case one hundred shares. Whenever possible, you should *trade in board lots* because there is a smaller spread between the bid and the ask, and they are more liquid. In response to your question as to the market on Bell, your broker might say: "It's thirty to a half, trading at a quarter." This means that the bid is thirty dollars, the ask is thirty dollars and fifty cents, and the last trade took place at thirty dollars and twenty-five cents. These different prices are due to the fact that the stock exchanges are *auction markets* where buyers and sellers haggle to get the best value. Indeed, despite the introduction of electronic equipment, floor traders on the exchanges still communicate by hand signals and transact their business by open outcry. On a busy day the floor of an exchange looks and sounds like a mob storming the Bastille.

You must now decide what price you are prepared to pay for

Bell. You can tell your broker to buy the shares at "market" which will guarantee that your order will be executed quickly, but you will probably pay the "ask" price. Or, you can stipulate any price you wish, *below* the asking price. If you stipulate a lower price you may pick up a relative bargain, but then again you may not buy the stock at all. My advice is, once you have made up your mind, *buy or sell at market,* providing the shares are actively traded. If a stock is an infrequent trader, there can be a wide discrepancy between the bid and the ask, which can result in you paying more or getting less than you should for it. For this reason I would also suggest that you stick to actively traded stocks, except for special situations.

There are other types of orders, which I will review briefly. You can stipulate a time limit, such as "good to the 2nd of May." This might be done when you want to receive the dividend on a stock that trades "ex-dividend" after that date. There are *three* dates to watch in connection with a dividend; the date on which it is paid, the record date (the date which the transfer agent uses to determine who will receive the dividend), and the ex-dividend date which the stock exchange uses to determine who qualifies for the dividend. You can also enter an "open" order that will stay in force for thirty days before it is cancelled. A "day" order is just that, it is good for one day.

You can stipulate "all or none" which means that unless the entire order can be filled at one swoop, it will not be executed. A "fill or kill" order means that the trader has a matter of minutes to execute it, and then the balance is cancelled. Unless you are trading in size and you don't want to disturb the market, there is no justification for this type of order. There are also "stop loss" and "stop buy" orders. Their purpose is to limit your loss by an automatic sale or purchase. Once a stock touches the "stop" price it becomes a market order, which means it may be filled *above or below* the last price. Finally, there are "contingent" orders where the purchase of one stock is contingent upon the sale of another stock, or vice versa, with a predetermined price spread between the two stocks. Contingent orders are tricky, and can cause floor traders heartburn.

Getting back to your purchase of two hundred shares of Bell, let us suppose you tell your broker to buy them at market. He will write out your order on a special blue form. (Blue forms are used for all buy orders, pink forms for all sell orders—the colour contrast is to help prevent mistakes, which can be hideously expensive.) The blue ticket is then given to the order clerk who enters it into a computer terminal. The computer checks the code, and routes it to the appropriate exchange where it is received at the firm's booth on the trading floor. A trader is called to the booth, given the ticket, and goes to the post where the stock is trading to execute the order.

Brokers with this automatic data processing system can fill orders from any of their branches across the country, on any major exchange, within a matter of *seconds* from the time the order enters the system.

As soon as your two hundred shares of Bell have been purchased, a wire is sent to the originating office. Your broker is then handed a time stamped copy of the order with the price paid for the shares on it. If he is a conscientious broker, he will immediately phone you to report that your order has been filled.

Before leaving the subject of entering an order, let me mention one more point. When buying or selling stocks always give the order to your broker as a number of shares, *not* a dollar value. For example, two hundred shares of Bell at thirty dollars would cost approximately six thousand dollars. You may think to yourself that you are buying six thousand worth of Bell, but to avoid confusion with your broker you must express it in terms of shares. If you have difficulty with math, your broker has a calculator and can figure it out for you. I have a client, a good friend, who gave me an order to buy "four thousand of Bank of Commerce warrants." I bought him four thousand warrants, and when he received his confirmation he nearly had a seizure. What he had meant was four thousand dollars *worth* of warrants. (The story has a happy ending, because he doubled his money on the warrants and now considers it a brilliant coup.) This shows what can happen when there is a misunderstanding. To make sure that your order is clear, have your broker *repeat it* back to you before you hang up the phone.

After you have bought or sold a security you will receive a written confirmation from your broker. A confirmation is the term used in the investment business for a bill or invoice. A typical stock confirmation appears on the next page.

BURNS FRY LIMITED / LIMITÉE

MEMBER
THE INVESTMENT DEALERS
ASSOCIATION OF CANADA AND
PRINCIPAL STOCK EXCHANGES IN CANADA

MEMBRE
L'ASSOCIATION CANADIENNE DES COURTIERS
EN VALEURS MOBILIÈRES ET ADHÉSIONS
BOURSIÈRES À TRAVERS LE CANADA

MEMBER
THROUGH SUBSIDIARY: NEW YORK,
AMERICAN, MIDWEST, PHILADELPHIA AND BOSTON
STOCK EXCHANGES IN THE UNITED STATES

MEMBRE
PAR L'ENTREMISE DE NOTRE FILIALE DE NEW YORK
AUPRÈS DES BOURSES AMÉRICAINES DU MIDWEST,
DE PHILADELPHIE, ET BOSTON

May 21, 1984

As agents, we confirm the following purchase for your account
on the Toronto Stock Exchange

200	Bell Enterprises Common	@ 30¼	
		Gross	$ 6,050.00
		Commission	84.20

NET AMOUNT $ 6,134.20

For settlement on May 28, 1984
at our office in Calgary

Mr. Joe Client
123 Anystreet
Wimola, Alberta
T1R 5B8

ACCOUNT NO.
F12 46-5130-5
A. Broker H2
Reg. Rep.
Reference 0123
Cusip 27683520
Sec # 548961

E. & O. E.   S. E. & O.

SEE REVERSE SIDE FOR CONDITIONS TO WHICH THIS TRANSACTION IS SUBJECT — VOIR AU VERSO LES CONDITIONS DE CETTE TRANSACTION.

You will notice that the confirmation shows the number of shares, whether they were bought or sold, a description of the security, the price of the security, and the amount of commission charged on the transaction. There are two dates on the confirmation: the transaction date (the day the order was executed) and the settlement date. The key date here is the *settlement* date. On or before this date you must pay the *total* shown on the invoice, or deliver the security you have sold. It is your responsibility, if you have done several transactions—such as a combination of buys and sells—to know how much you owe, and to pay that amount. If you have trouble sorting out the net amount, your broker will help you out. (If he is surly about extending this service you should find yourself another broker.) The settlement date applies to *both* the client and the broker. When you sell securities, the broker must pay *you* on that date.

Should you fail to pay for the security on settlement date, or fail to deliver a security that you have sold, the broker has the legal right to sell you out or buy you in. This means that he can sell the shares you have not paid for, or buy back the shares you have sold. He would do this to avoid financial loss, because the broker is acting as your agent and must make good on the transaction with another party. In the event of a "sell out" or "buy in" the client bears the expense. Most brokers will go to great lengths to avoid selling out or buying in a client—but they have the right to do it.

The settlement date varies with the type of security. Listed stocks settle *five business days* after the transaction date, as do most unlisted stocks and many bonds. Options settle *one* business day after the trade, some bonds settle *two* days after the transaction and Treasury Bills can settle the *same* or the *following* day. If you're in doubt, ask the broker *before* you do the deal and after you have done it check your confirmation.

New issues are an entirely different kettle of fish. A new issue, be it bonds or shares, can settle up to four or five weeks from the date of the transaction. Another peculiarity about new issues, which confuses many people, is the phrase "If as and when" which is printed on most confirmations. This is a standard wording which for all intents and purposes can be ignored. It is used to protect the underwriters in the unlikely event that there is a hitch—such as a legal or financial problem—which forces them to delay or cancel the issue. But this is most unusual. By the time you receive your confirmation, even though it says "if as and when issued," you are on the hook.

You do, however, have one legitimate avenue of escape. This is your Right of Rescission. When you receive your new issue confirmation you will also receive a prospectus. A prospectus is a legal document that provides comprehensive information on the issue. If there is a false or misleading statement in the prospectus, you can exercise your right of rescission and rescind (cancel) the contract. You will rarely be given this opportunity because corporate lawyers pore over each prospectus—and are challenged on the tiniest technicality by the securities commissions—until the prospectus is literally letter perfect. A prospectus can be a most revealing document, and should be read *before* you commit yourself to buying a new issue. It may be impossible to obtain a final or definitive prospectus before the issue is spoken for by investors, but you can usually get a *preliminary* prospectus from your broker. This document, which is known in the trade as a "red herring" is essentially the same as the final prospectus except that certain vital figures are missing—figures that pertain to the pricing and yield of the issue. One of the oldest maxims in the business is "investigate before you invest." This may sound trite, but it makes sense.

When you buy a stock or a bond and instruct that it be registered in your name, this will be done *after* you pay for it. Delivery of the certificate can take up to five or six weeks. The reason for this delay is that the certificate is issued by the company's transfer agent, which is normally a trust company. Trust companies are not noted for their speed. However, from the transaction date (the day you bought the security) you are the beneficial owner and this means that you can sell it any time you want, even though you have not received the certificate.

The most common problem when a client sells a security is "good delivery" of the certificate. Good delivery means that the certificate must not only be on time, but in negotiable form for transfer by the broker. If the security is registered in your name the certificate must be *signed* on the back, before it can be considered good delivery. This can also be accomplished in your absence if you sign a power of attorney form, which is subsequently attached to the certificate. Never *ever* sign a power of attorney that does not specify the security *and* the certificate number. And always get a receipt when you deliver a certificate.

A stock certificate is an interesting piece of paper. The more expensive ones are engraved and printed with special inks, and have the feel of a banknote. (This is not surprising, because in Canada most certificates are made by the two principal banknote companies.) Certificates often contain a vignette of one or more human forms, typically a muscular man or a voluptuous woman in clinging robes. This is not cheesecake, but a device to foil counterfeiters because it is almost impossible to reproduce the subtle flesh tones and the texture of cloth in a steel engraving. On the opposite page is an illustration of a stock certificate.

Some securities come in "bearer form" which means that they are *not* registered in your name (Treasury Bills are one example) and do not need your signature. This type of certificate, or one that has previously been signed off, is as negotiable as a bank-note, and should be treated with the same care. Whatever type of certificate you present to your broker, it must be in good condition. If your dog has chewed it, or the baby has vomited on it, it will *not* be considered good delivery.

Certificates should always be kept in a safe place. Yet many people treat them casually, and leave them around the house. If a certificate is lost or stolen it is sometimes possible to replace it, but this is a long and expensive process involving the purchase of an indemnity bond. The best thing to do with your certificates is to place them in a safety deposit box or to leave them with your broker. Normally, brokers do not charge for safekeeping, but they usually insist that the securities be held in the firm's name. The advantage of leaving certificates with your broker is the convenience. You do not have to come in to make deliveries, and the broker collects all dividends and interest on your behalf. At the end of the year, the broker sends you a T-5 form for tax purposes. There are some disadvantages. When a broker holds your securities, you may not receive annual or quarterly reports from the companies, and there is also an element of risk. If an employee takes off to Rio de Janeiro with your securities, the firm's insurance will probably cover your loss. But if the firm goes belly up, you could be in trouble. I should add that if thieves tunneled into your bank and removed the contents of

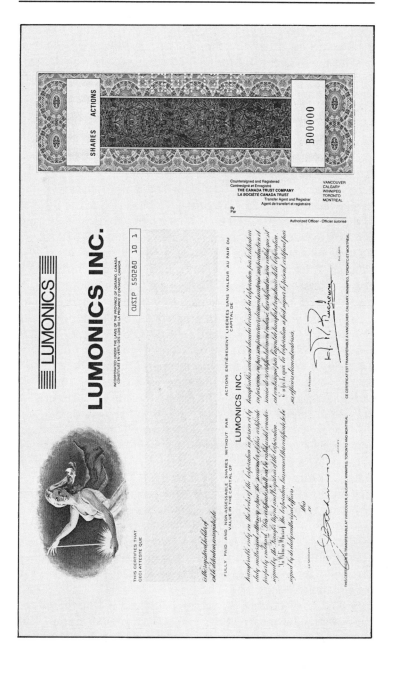

your safety deposit box, you would have an equally serious problem. Notwithstanding these hazards, a bank or a brokerage firm is a much safer place for securities than your bureau drawer.

If you invest on margin, you will have no choice as to who will keep your securities—your broker will hold them as collateral. There are some things you should know about margin. First, buying on margin means that you are playing with *borrowed* money. This gives you leverage on your investments. The advantage of leverage is that it can magnify your winnings. But leverage is a two-edged sword, and works *both* ways. Leverage can also magnify your losses. The principle behind margin is that the broker lends you a stated percentage of the value of the security at the outset of the transaction. You pay the broker interest, and put up the balance. If the stock falls in value, the broker's loan *declines* with the price of the shares, and *you must make up the difference*. If the stock rises in price, you build up a credit which you may take out in cash, or use to finance another purchase.

Before you can invest on margin, you must sign a Margin Agreement with the broker. Regardless of which firm you choose, the wording is similar—and odious—in all margin agreements. Normally, there are ten to fifteen clauses in a Margin Agreement. The clause that most people choke at permits the broker *at his discretion* to sell them out, or to buy them in, *without notice*. In fact, brokers rarely resort to this clause, and only do so to protect themselves *and* the client in a dangerous situation. Indeed, brokers encourage margin accounts for two reasons. First, a client on margin generates more commissions, because he is playing with more money. Secondly, the broker makes a profit on the loan to the client. (The rate of interest charged by the broker is usually one per cent more than the firm pays to borrow from the bank.) I have had a number of lawyers phone me indignantly and say that they would not sign a Margin Agreement. I never argue with them, but tell them if they don't sign, they can't invest on margin. After shopping around for a less onerous contract, they usually sign and we get on with their business.

The margin requirement is always stated as a percentage, which the client must put up, either in cash or securities. The percentage varies with the perceived risk of the security and its price. Thus some short Canada bonds may be purchased for as little as three per cent margin while low priced stocks may require eighty per cent margin. A typical rate for a stock listed on the Toronto exchange is fifty per cent margin. Using this rate, here is an example of how margin works:

Client buys 200 shares @$20		cost $4000
Broker's loan to client 50%	$2000	
Client puts up 50%	$2000	
	$4000	$4000

If the shares decline to fifteen dollars, the client will receive a "margin call" and have to put up an additional five hundred dollars, as the following figures will show:

Value of original shares now	$3000	cost $4000
Broker's loan (50% of $3000)	$1500	
Client's original deposit	$2000	
	$3500	$4000
Additional margin required	$ 500	

Had the shares risen in price to twenty-five dollars, the client would have had *excess* margin in his account and could have withdrawn up to five hundred dollars.

Value of original shares now	$5000	cost $4000
Broker's loan (50% of $5000)	$2500	
Client's original deposit	$2000	
	$4500	$4000
Excess available to client	$ 500	

Now that you know how margin works, I should tell you that not all securities are marginable, and not all brokers offer margin to their clients. The exchanges and regulatory bodies set the *minimum* margin requirements, but a firm can set higher requirements if it wishes, and can also decide what securities it is prepared to finance on margin. I get criticized from time to time because the firm I work for has relatively high margin requirements, and it looks with a jaundiced eye at some stocks on the Vancouver Exchange. We lose business as a result of this stringent policy, but it helps to keep our clients solvent so they can play another day.

Margin accounts are monitored by the exchanges and the Investment Dealers Association. If a broker permits clients to trade with insufficient margin, the firm is subject to heavy fines. It is for this reason that brokers constantly watch their margin accounts and issue "margin calls" when clients are under margin. A margin call is a demand for more money—usually by telephone or telegram—and the client must respond *immediately*. Both brokers and clients loathe margin calls. Jesse Livermore, the legendary Wall Street plunger who at one stage in his career had direct lines to thirty brokers, had this to say of margin calls: "I know but one sure tip from a broker. It is your margin call. When it reaches you, close your account. You are on the wrong side of the market."

Most unlisted stocks are not marginable. The unlisted market is really a floating crap game in that it has no premises, and transactions are done over the telephone between dealers. Trades on the exchanges are done by *auction*, but on the unlisted market trades are done by *negotiation*. It is difficult to regulate the unlisted market and it is also difficult to keep track of what is happening there. These factors produce so much risk that it is too dangerous for margin purposes. Except for newly issued shares of senior companies that are about to be listed on an exchange, I would avoid *all* unlisted stocks.

Margin is also required when you make a short sale. The purpose of a short sale is to profit when a stock goes *down* in price. Margin is needed because you sell shares that you don't own, and the broker must borrow them for you. The way a short sale works is that you sell the shares at a given price and when they decline your buy them back (cover your short position) at a lower price. The difference between what you sold them for, and the price you paid to buy them back, is your profit.

There is nothing unethical about a short sale, in fact it is a good way to make money. But there are certain restrictions and hazards. When you make a short sale, you must first ask your broker if he can borrow the stock for you. Assuming he can, he must mark "short sale" on the order. This means that your trade can not be executed at a lower price than the previous sale. (The exchanges have this rule to prevent a stock being hammered into the ground by short sellers—which is known as a "bear raid.") Having sold short, you may be forced to buy your shares back if the lender demands delivery of his stock. Your maximum profit on a short sale is the price you sold it for. However, if the stock should go *up* your potential loss is *limitless*. The margin required on a short sale varies with the price of the stock, but is high. If you want to play stocks on the downside, you are much better off to buy "put" options. This will be discussed in a later chapter.

The great appeal of margin is that it allows you to play with more chips, but margin is *only* for experienced investors. I have seen novices wiped out as a result of margin. Ronald was one who sticks in my memory. He wasn't a client of mine, but he was in our office frequently. In those days we had a boardroom with rows of chairs where clients could sit and watch the Trans Lux tape. At lunch hour the room would be filled with a motley assortment, some of whom I am sure only came in to escape the weather. Ronald stood out in the crowd because he looked so fit and so prosperous. He was in his mid-thirties at that time, and owned a successful business. Then a mining market developed and Ronald discovered margin. Soon he was fully invested. As the weeks went by, some of Ronald's stocks went up, but most of them went down. This triggered repeated margin calls. Ronald should have heeded Jesse Livermore's advice and closed his account. Instead, he scraped up more money and grimly hung on. Eventually, he was forced to sell off his stocks one by one. During this period Ronald went into a severe physical and mental decline. When I last saw him, his face was haggard and his skin was the colour of putty. He later went bankrupt.

Ronald's experience shows the negative aspect of margin. Remember, if you gamble with borrowed money and *lose*, the consequences can be most unpleasant.

CHAPTER 4

Sources of Information and Advice

THE SECURITIES MARKETS feed on news and react quickly to it. Throughout the day on Wall Street and on Bay Street, the tom toms beat incessantly. The messages they send are not always accurate—quite often they are just rumours—but the effect is the same. As an investor, you owe it to yourself to know what is happening. If you don't, it can cost you money. With apologies to Rudyard Kipling, if you can keep your head while all around you are losing theirs—you probably haven't heard the news.

One way to keep informed is to read a good newspaper. Having started in the investment business in Montreal, I began by reading *The Gazette*. Later, when I was transferred to Ottawa, I read both *The Gazette* and *The Globe and Mail*. Eventually, I didn't have time to read both papers and I chose *The Globe and Mail*. (The *Globe* is printed simultaneously in a number of locations, thus you can get same day delivery in most cities.) I don't hold any brief for *The Globe and Mail* but its Report on Business section is, in my opinion, the best in Canada.

Aside from my personal preference, it is only fair to add that *The Toronto Star*, *The Vancouver Sun*, and my old favourite, *The Gazette*, also have excellent financial sections. All three will keep you well informed.

For investors whose main interest is the American market, one newspaper stands out above all the rest—*The Wall Street Journal*. It should need no introduction. *The Wall Street Journal* contains masses of information and is noted for its superb editorials. The only drawback for Canadians is that in most parts of the country, *The Wall Street Journal* arrives several days late.

There are also two financial newspapers published weekly in Canada. They are *The Financial Post* and the *Financial Times*. *The Financial Post* covers the entire business spectrum and is a voluminous publication. Because *The Financial Post* addresses such a wide audience it contains a lot of information that is not relevant to the market. My only complaint, speaking as a broker, is that I have to wade through a lot of chaff to find the wheat. Sometimes it's worth the effort. It is also the most prestigious financial paper in the country—so if you want to impress your friends at the office you might subscribe to *The Financial Post*.

The *Financial Times* is a smaller paper with a more concise format. It has some fine writers and some features, such as a monthly performance ranking of mutual funds, that make it well worth reading. One of the things I like best about the *Financial Times* is that when I'm busy, I can skim through it in a few minutes.

The Northern Miner is a venerable weekly that caters to investors and the mining industry. Its chief value is that it tells you what is going on in the field and in the mining markets. It is not a source of hot market tips. By the time news appears in *The Northern Miner*—or any other newspaper—you can be sure that it has already been discounted in the price of the stock. Nevertheless, if you invest in mining stocks, you will be better informed if you read *The Northern Miner*.

Another publication that deserves mention is the *Investor's Digest of Canada*. As its name implies, it is aimed directly at investors. It comes out every two weeks and is published by *The Financial Post*. There is something in the *Investor's Digest* for everyone. The front page is devoted to a column on the general market. Inside there are in-depth company studies and forecasts (culled from various brokers) on corporate earnings. Frank Kaplan, former mining editor of *The Financial Post*, has a column on the mining and metal sector. Two other columns of interest to speculators are the "Oil Patch Dispatch" by a well-informed pundit who signs himself "Percy," and "West of the Rockies" which deals with the Vancouver Exchange. The *Investor's Digest* is twice as expensive as *The Post* or the *Times*, but in my opinion it is a good buy.

Business magazines can be useful to investors, but mostly for background information. In this country the best is *Canadian Business*. In the United States the leading magazines are *Barron's*, *Business Week*, *Forbe's*, and *Fortune*. All are good.

There are also a host of "market letters" available to the public. A market letter is a periodical that provides advice on investments. They differ widely in quality and content. To receive a market letter you have to subscribe to it. Sometimes the cost of the subscription can be deducted as an investment expense. Don't take my word for it—check with your accountant.

Legitimate market letters should *not* be confused with brochures sent out by stock promoters. These fly-by-night operators imitate the same format as a market letter, and usually begin by discussing senior resource stocks. This is to lull you into a false sense of security. Then mention is made of a major discovery by a company such as Noranda. (Noranda is a favourite because Noranda has mines all over the place.) Now get ready for it, here comes the dart. A mere seven hundred miles north of the discovery, a *similar* orebody has been found by Old Moose Pasture Mines. The rest of the market letter goes on to extoll the virtues of Old Moose Pasture, and urges you to buy its shares. This type of market letter should be filed in the wastebasket.

In the eyes of the public, Joesph Granville is the most famous author of a market letter. Joe Granville attained astounding prominence from 1980 to 1982. In the final stages of the Bull Market his pronouncements had such effect that stocks he recommended would be delayed in trading because of the influx of buy orders. With uncanny precision he predicted the top of the market, and told his subscribers to sell all their stocks. The market fell, and continued to do so for many months. Everyone held their breath and waited for Joe to tell them when to buy again. Joe boasted that when he gave a buy signal, there would be such a stampede that the exchanges would have to close. But Joe never gave a buy signal. Even after the market reached bottom in August of 1982, and prices started to rise again. Indeed, Joe told his disciples that it was a false rally and to *short* the market. This proved to be most unfortunate, because in the next sixteen months, the Dow Jones Industrial Average rose five hundred points. Those that followed Granville's advice lost a fortune. Joe lost his reputation for infallibility, and many of his subscribers.

As this book goes to press Joe Granville is still a bear, and for the past eight months he has been quite right to maintain this stance. Even so, it is unlikely that he will ever again be regarded, as he once was, as the greatest stock market guru in the world. *The Granville Market Letter* can be entertaining to read because Joe pulls no punches, and he writes with absolute conviction. He is also a colourful and amusing speaker. I have read his letter and I have heard him speak—and find that a little bit of Granville goes a long way.

In the United States there are scores of investment publications. If I was to choose one, it would be the *Value Line*. The *Value Line* is more of an investment service than a market letter, although you receive weekly installments which you retain in a binder. This service covers approximately sixteen hundred companies, most of which are listed on U.S. exchanges. Each company is summarized on a single page which includes a chart of the stock, statistics, a description and opinion of the company, as well as a rating on its timeliness and safety. All this information is updated on a regular basis. The *Value Line* has a solid reputation and a good batting average on its recommendations. Over the years I have found it to be excellent.

Canadian market letters range from *Third Wave Investing*, which deals exclusively with "high tech" companies, to the *George Cross Newsletter*, which consists mainly of press releases from junior resource companies. Rather than trying to plough through the entire list, I will mention three market letters that you might consider.

The oldest is *The Investment Reporter*, formerly *Canadian Business Service*. It is published each week, and offers sound but unspectacular advice. Its chief appeal is to the conservative investor who owns, or is interested in acquiring, a portfolio of better quality securities. You won't get rich quick by following

The Investment Reporter, but then again you won't get into any serious trouble.

The main methods used to forecast prices are *fundamental* analysis and *technical* analysis. These two methods will be explained later in the book, but why I mention them is that one of the most successful proponents of technical analysis is a Canadian named Ian McAvity. He publishes a bi-monthly market letter called *Deliberations.* This letter covers a wide range of topics including interest rates, currencies, precious metals, and stocks. *Deliberations* is aimed at the sophisticated investor. Among those who subscribe to it are institutions and individuals all over the world.

McAvity is not a show business personality, but he has appeared on "Wall Street Week" and other programs a number of times. He clashed with Dr. Morton Shulman one night when he was a guest on Shulman's television show. While they were on the air Shulman bet McAvity one thousand dollars that the price of gold would go up rather than down. McAvity proved to be right. To his credit, Shulman paid McAvity the thousand dollars when he next appeared on "The Shulman File."

This leads me to my third recommendation, *The Money Letter.* It is published weekly, and has a big circulation in Canada. *The Money Letter* consists of specific investment recommendations by a panel of experts. These include Ian McAvity, Dr. Morton Shulman, and Andrew Sarlos. Shulman—who has been incredibly successful in the market—is the main drawing card. Andrew Sarlos used to share equal billing with Shulman until HCI Holdings came a cropper. Sarlos built his reputation with HCI Holdings, a company which he controlled. The stock of HCI went from ninety cents in 1978 to over nineteen dollars in 1981. However, in 1982, HCI's balance sheet turned into a disaster area and the shares plummeted to forty-seven cents.

The Money Letter also has a tax expert, David Louis, who comments on tax shelters and similar topics. Most of the investment recommendations in *The Money Letter* make good sense, and a fair percentage turn out to be winners. But not all of them, therefore some judgement is required on your part. Shulman and McAvity are the two who command my attention, and whom I read very carefully. Shulman is particularly good on currency trading, but I would interject a word of caution. Most of his currency recommendations involve a high degree of leverage, which means that if they go sour you can lose your *entire* investment. Aside from this *caveat*, I would say that *The Money Letter* is an excellent choice for the average investor.

Turning away from market letters, we now come to investment counselling firms. Investment counselling firms should *not* be confused with money management companies. The latter are usually not qualified to advise on the securities markets, and they often sell mortgages or mutual funds. Investment counsellors, on the other hand, are licenced to give advice on a broad range of securities and do not sell anything other than their expertise. For a fee, investment counsellors will advise you on your holdings, or manage your entire portfolio. There are investment counselling firms in Toronto, Montreal, and Vancouver as well as a number of other Canadian cities.

Investment counsellors are not for small investors as the *minimum* account they will accept runs from one hundred to five hundred thousand dollars. Their fees are on a sliding scale, based on the size of the account; most charge a fee of around one per cent for the first million, and lesser percentages above that amount. Some of the best investment counselling firms only advise pension funds and institutions. If you have a sizeable portfolio and don't want to manage it yourself, you should consider the services of an investment counsellor. As with every other type of business, some are better than others—so ask around before you make a commitment.

Portfolio management is also available from some of the integrated investment houses. For a similar fee you can get the same services that are provided by investment counselling firms. If you choose to have your portfolio managed professionally by a broker, you should be aware of two potential problems. The first is that being a broker, the firm may "churn" your holdings (trade them too frequently) to generate large commissions. The second is that being underwriters, the firm might slug your account full of new issues that it was unable to sell to other clients. Both have happened in the past, but in my opinion there is very little risk of these problems occurring today.

Depending on the size of your account you can pay a trust

company to manage your portfolio. This would make sense if you decide to place all your assets in the hands of one custodian. A trust company—for a handsome fee—will look after your financial needs while you live, and administer your estate after you die. It would not, however, be a good idea if you want aggressive performance from your portfolio, because trust companies are by nature conservative investors.

Now we come to free advice, and there's lots of it around. Among the sources of free investment tips are hairdressers, bartenders, gas station attendants, Uncle George, people at cocktail parties, Aunt Becky, your brother-in-law, and sundry friends. If properly approached, you can also get free investment advice from your clergyman, lawyer, doctor, and bank manager. Ignore them all. Especially your bank manager. Stop for a minute and ask yourself what a bank manager is good at, other than saying "no." Reflect upon this question, and give it some serious thought. Now that you have thought about it, why would you ask your bank manager for investment advice?

I deliberately did not mention another source of free advice— your broker. The bad part about asking your broker for investment advice is that he might end up selling you something. Having got that out of the way, you will have to admit that he is the logical person to speak to, because the market is his business. If your broker doesn't know the answer to a question, he can ask someone in his research department. (Research analysts spend most of their time ferreting out information.) Your broker is the only person who can give you up to the minute reports on the market. In addition to his video terminal, which is connected to the exchanges, he gets a constant flow of news from the Dow-Jones machine (which garners information from all over the world), and he also receives research bulletins on the Telex. It should be added that your broker has a strong incentive to give you good advice. If he gives you bad advice, he may lose your account. But if he can make money for you, you will do more business with him. Not only that, you may recommend him to your friends.

Many people feel that it is impossible to make big money in the market unless you have inside information. The accepted belief is that to get inside information you must have a friend who is a corporate bigwig or be sitting beside your broker when he receives a call from an insider. It is further suggested that if you don't live within spitting distance of Wall Street or Bay Street, you are beyond the pale and haven't got a chance. This is not true. Let me tell you about Victor.

Victor has been a client of mine for years. He is a retired public servant, and lives on the outskirts of Ottawa. One day in 1979 a man came to his door, who was selling cemetery plots. This was a longer term investment than Victor cared to make, but he asked the man in for a cup of coffee. They chatted about the cemetery business, and Victor learned that it was booming. (The reason for this phenomenon is that in North America we have an aging population.) After the salesman left, Victor hustled down to the public library and looked up the financial information on the cemetery company. He noted with interest that it had cemeteries across Canada and its earnings were in a steady uptrend. The name of the company was Arbor Capital, and its shares were listed on the Toronto Stock Exchange.

Because the shares of Arbor Capital traded infrequently, Victor bought two thousand at $1.07 which was the offering price. Over the next year he left open orders in to buy more at higher prices, and eventually acquired a total of twelve thousand shares. His average cost came to $2.31 per share. Most of this stock he placed in his Registered Retirement Savings Plan to shelter it from capital gains tax. This was a prudent move, because the shares of Arbor Capital rose dramatically and were split in 1982. By 1983, the shares that had cost him $2.31 were each worth more than $25. On paper, he had a tax-sheltered profit of $275,000. Victor is still holding Arbor Capital, and he's very happy with it. He had no inside information on the company—but he was smart enough to recognize an investment opportunity when it knocked on his door.

Investors can also tune in to radio and television programs that give daily market reports. Some of the Canadian television programs are particularly good. Because they originate in Canada, don't sell them short.

The most popular television program on investments is "Wall Street Week," which is shown on the American PBS network each Friday. I have watched "Wall Street Week" for years and find it entertaining. Initially, I thought that I would learn what was *really* happening in the American market, and pick up priceless pearls of wisdom. Alas, what I discovered was that some of the special guests knew what they were talking about, and some did not. My problem was to know who I should believe, and this stumped me. What I did conclude was that the regular panelists, who appear every Friday, are consistently *wrong* in their assessment of the market.

I remember one program in particular. It was in the autumn of 1979, and I had come home from the office deeply worried that the market was in for a major decline. It had been an ominous week on the exchanges. I watched "Wall Street Week" that night to see what the panelists had to say. Not only did all three regulars state that the worst was yet to come, but the "elves" (the show's technical indicator) also said that the market was going to hell in a basket. This is what I had hoped to hear. That night I slept soundly for the first time in days.

The following Monday the market turned around and prices started moving up again. I wasn't surprised in the least. Having heard the predictions on "Wall Street Week," I was confident this would happen.

CHAPTER 5

Bonds

I BEGAN MY securities career as an apple-cheeked bond salesman. In those days bonds were an important part of the investment scene. It might surprise you to know that they still are. The reason is that the bond market is tied to interest rates, and interest rates profoundly affect the stock market. So, even if you consider bonds a bore, I suggest you read this chapter.

What is a bond? A bond is a promissory note with a specified face value and a term of from one to thirty years. When you buy a bond you *lend* the issuer your money for a stated period. In return, the borrower pays you a fixed rate of interest during that period, and when the time is up you get your money back. The amount you receive at the end of the term is the face value on the certificate. Interest is paid to you, usually twice a year, by cheque or by coupons attached to the certificate.

Bond prices rise and fall with interest rates. The relationship between the prevailing interest rate and a bond is the same as a see-saw. When interest *rates go up, bond prices go down.* Conversely, when interest *rates fall, bond prices rise.* The reason for this is simple.

Let us assume that the prevailing interest rate for a bond that matures in ten years is twelve per cent. This means that people with money to invest can buy ten-year bonds paying them twelve per cent. Now suppose you have a ten-year bond to sell with a face value of one thousand dollars which pays only eight per cent or eighty dollars a year. If you ask one thousand dollars for that bond, no one will touch it. Eight per cent is less than the going rate. However, *if you reduce the price* of the bond sufficiently, the yield will equal twelve per cent—and you will be able to sell it. Figuring out the discount is done by a mathematical formula, but there is no need for you to do it, the investment dealer will do it for you. Here is the bottom line:

> bond pays $80 per year which at $1000 yields 8%
> but if it is discounted to <u>$770</u>
> a 10-year bond paying $80 per year yields <u>12%</u>

Therefore, to sell your bond at a competitive price, you would have to discount it to $770. (Bonds normally have a face value of $1000, but dealers always express the price in $100 units, thus $770 would be referred to as 77). By the same token, if the prevailing interest rate for ten-year bonds was to drop to six per cent, your bond would go *up* in value. Under this scenario, people with money to invest would have to be satisfied with six per cent. You would be in the fortunate position of owning a bond that was selling at a premium, or an amount greater than its face value. In this case, 115. For this situation, here is the bottom line:

> bond pays $80 per year which at $1000 yields 8%
> if the price is increased to <u>$1150</u>
> 10-year bond paying $80 per year yields 6%

The return on a bond, which consists of its coupon *plus any discount* or *minus any premium*, is known as its "yield to maturity." Most often, it is simply referred to as the yield. Yield is critical to the price of a bond, because the bond market marches to the tune of interest rates, thus yields are constantly changing. As we have seen, when the yield changes on a bond, *so does the price of the bond.*

You can make money on bonds by buying them when interest

rates are falling, or by selling (shorting) them when interest rates are on the rise. The average person hears little about the bond market, because bond trading takes place "over-the-counter" rather than on the stock exchanges. Strictly speaking, it is part of the unlisted market in that transactions are done by negotiation, and trades take place over a network of direct telephone lines. But it is a much more liquid market, and the participants differ from those who trade unlisted stocks. In Canada, about one hundred investment dealers as well as trust companies and banks trade bonds. The Bank of Canada is also a major player in this game. In 1983, the trading value in the bond market totalled about four hundred *billion*, or more than ten times the combined value of all trades on Canada's stock exchanges.

Bonds are categorized as being long term, mid term, or short term. Long term bonds have a maturity of more than ten years, mid term are those that mature between three and ten years, and short term bonds mature in less than three years. Normally, the longer the term of the bond, the higher the yield. The reason for higher yields on long term bonds is not only due to the "rental" factor on long term money, but also to compensate the lender for the increased risk of insolvency, the erosion of his capital from inflation, and the possibility of a further rise in interest rates. When comparing bonds of a similar quality, but of differing maturities, a "yield curve" can be drawn on a piece of paper. A normal yield curve, an example of which appears on page 52, resembles the flight path of a jumbo-jet making its departure.

When the economy overheats and short term rates rise above long term rates, you get an *inverted* yield curve. An inverted yield curve—also illustrated on page 52—spells trouble.

This condition is unnatural and unsustainable, because the lender obtains a higher return on a lesser risk. An inverted yield curve *is bad news for everyone.* When it is in force, funds are sucked out of the long term bond market *and* the stock market by the lure of higher returns with reduced risk in the short term market. As a result, *both the bond and the stock markets go into a decline.*

NORMAL YIELD CURVE

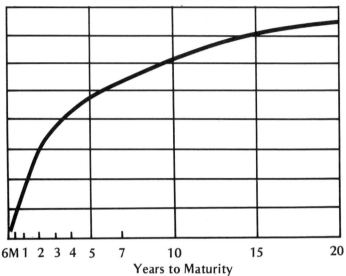

Years to Maturity

INVERTED YIELD CURVE

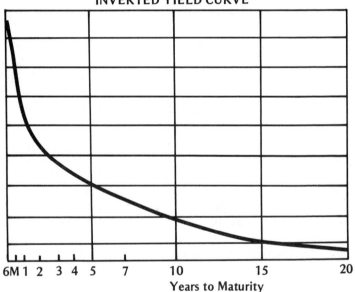

Years to Maturity

The important thing to remember about a yield curve is that the yields are insignificant, what counts is their *relationship to each other*. In other words, you can have a normal yield curve during a period of relatively high rates and an inverted curve when rates are historically low. If you wish, you can make a simple yield curve diagram for yourself. Just look at the "Bond Prices" column in *The Globe and Mail* and note down a selection of Government of Canada bonds, with their maturity dates and yields. For a quick check, all you will need is four or five. The bellweather issues in the long term are Canada 9½% due 2001, and Canada 10¼% due 2004. For a mid term bond you might choose Canada 11% due 1989. In the short end you could use Canada 10% due 1986, and the latest issue of 91 day Treasury Bills.

Treasury Bills are short term notes—usually with a term of 91 or 182 days—which the Bank of Canada auctions every Thursday. They are bought by investment dealers, banks, and other financial institutions. The average yield of the 91 day Bills is used to set the Bank Rate, which is always twenty-five basis points above the average yield of the Bills. (A "basis point" is one hundredth of one per cent, therefore twenty-five basis points is one quarter of one per cent.) The Bank Rate is the rate of interest at which the Bank of Canada will lend money to the chartered banks. It is significant to the public because most of the chartered banks add about one per cent to the Bank Rate to arrive at *their* Prime Rate—the rate of interest they will charge to their best customers.

By putting in its own bid for all or part of the Treasury Bill issue, the Bank of Canada can manipulate interest rates. In fact, it can play the rates like a piano. In addition, by buying and selling in the open market it can ease or restrict the money supply. When the Bank of Canada buys bonds, it pumps money into the system. Bond prices rise and interest rates decline. When it is a heavy seller, it restricts the money supply (because the dealers pay the Bank of Canada) and bond prices decline. Interest rates of course rise. Rigging the market is a legitimate function of the central bank. It is also done to stabilize the value of the Canadian dollar. If interest rates in Canada are not kept above those in the United States, money will leave Canada for deposit at a higher rate across the border. When this happens, investors sell Canadian dollars and buy U.S. dollars. As a result of the selling, the Canadian dollar falls in price.

Treasury Bills are peculiar in that they do not pay interest but are sold at a discount. For tax purposes, however, the discount is treated as interest. Your return is derived from the difference between the discount and the maturity price, which is one hundred or "par." For instance if you bought Treasury Bills maturing in 91 days to yield 9½%, you would pay 97.686 or $976.86 per thousand. On maturity you would receive one thousand dollars of which $23.14 ($1000.00 — $976.86) would represent the discount, or your interest. By the same token, if you bought a Treasury Bill maturing in 30 days on a 9½% yield basis, you would pay 99.225 or $992.25 per thousand. In this example, your "interest" for 30 days would come to $7.75. Because of their safety and liquidity, Treasury Bills are a useful place to park short term funds. You can buy them from your broker or your bank.

Another feature I should mention about Treasury Bills is that they come in "bearer form" and hence are as negotiable as a dollar bill. For this reason, it is best to leave them with your bank or broker for safekeeping. This reminds me of my early days with Royal Securities in Ottawa. At that time there were only two of us in the office, the manager and myself. We used to take turns going to the Bank of Canada on Wellington Street to pick up Treasury Bills. In those days mugging was not a major sport, so we were pretty casual about security precautions. Not only did we go alone, but we walked the six or eight blocks back to the office with the Treasury Bills stuffed under our shirts. One summer day I picked up three million dollars worth of Treasury Bills from the Bank of Canada—I remember they were in one hundred thousand dollar denominations—and after stuffing them under my shirt I started back to the office. As I was marching up Sparks Street the wad of certificates shifted, and to my horror about a million dollars worth slipped down my pant leg and out onto the pavement. Fortunately none were lost, but I had some anxious moments counting them. Since that incident I have treated Treasury Bills with considerably more care.

The Bank of Canada also dominates the market for new issues of bonds. Government of Canada bonds are underwritten by investment dealers and subsequently sold to institutions and the public. The timing of these offerings is basically whenever the government needs money. Some Canada issues are Retractable or Extendible. If a bond is retractable, the bondholder can retract or cash his bonds at a specific time *prior* to the maturity date. If it is extendible, the bondholder has the right to extend the maturity for a fixed period. Both are attractive features. Government of Canada bonds provide the greatest safety of principal and the best liquidity to investors. However, they fluctuate with interest rates, the same as any other bonds.

One of the most memorable issues was the Canada Conversion Loan which came out in the autumn of 1958. The purpose of this issue was to refinance a host of maturing Victory Loan Bonds that Canadian investors had bought during the war. It was the largest bond issue ever floated in Canada, and the government took pains to enlist the support of the investment community to put it over. I remember attending a huge gathering of investment dealers in Montreal, in the Royal Bank building, where we were addressed on closed circuit television by Donald Fleming, the Minister of Finance. Mr. Fleming, who was in his shirtsleeves, exhorted us for the sake of Canada to persuade everyone who held Victory Bonds to exchange them for the Conversion Loan bonds. Imbued with patriotic zeal we went out and did just that. Most of us felt that we were part of a national crusade, and doing our country and the public a great service.

In fact, at the behest of the government, we gave the public a royal screwing. After the Conversion Loan was floated, the Bank of Canada supported the bonds for a short period of time, and then withdrew its bid. The three issues immediately fell with a thump, and never recovered. The long term part of the loan, which was a 4½% bond maturing in 1983 went as low as sixty-seven. I relate this story to drive home the point that the value of any bond is subject to the prevailing interest rates. Even a Government of Canada bond.

The only Government of Canada issues that are an exception to this rule are Canada Savings Bonds. These are offered to the public once each year, usually in November. The great advantage of these bonds is that they can be redeemed at *any time* at *full face value*, without charge. The amount you are allowed to buy is limited, and the rate of interest is lower than non-redeemable bonds of a similar maturity. Also they are non-transferable (you can't sell them to anyone else) so it is impossible to make a profit on them. Nevertheless, Canada Savings Bonds are an excellent investment because of their safety and liquidity, and I would highly recommend them. Indeed, a Canada Savings Bond is the only security a broker can sell with the certain knowledge that his client won't lose money—except through inflation.

I consider bonds a poor long term investment because of inflation, and the fact that bond interest is fully taxable. If you want to *speculate* in bonds stick to Government of Canada issues. The reason I say this is that Canada bonds are the most marketable, hence you can buy and sell them in quantity. If you are going to trade bonds you should know that the action is in the long term end, which has the biggest swings. Also, low coupon bonds tend to fluctuate more widely than high coupon bonds. Because the price fluctuations are *relatively* small, you should trade in sizeable amounts. It is one area where it makes sense to trade on margin. The margin requirement on some Canada bonds is as low as two or three per cent.

People are frequently confused as to whether they hold a Canada Savings Bond or a "regular" Government of Canada bond. One way to tell is to read the face of the certificate. As a convenience, Canada Savings Bonds are smaller than normal size certificates. Because reproducing an actual certificate is a criminal offence, opposite is a facsimile of a Canada Savings Bond.

The provinces also issue bonds from time to time, and there are a great many provincial issues outstanding. Provincial bonds yield a little more than Government of Canada bonds due to the higher credit risk. In addition, the yields differ among the provinces for the same reason. Two companies, Canadian Bond Rating Service of Montreal and Dominion Bond Rating Service of Toronto, publish credit ratings on debt issues, including those of the provinces. In most cases bonds guaranteed by the province (such as Ontario Hydro) get a similar rating to the province. Sometimes, the bond market has a different perception of the credit ratings and this is reflected in the prices the market will pay. The judgement that *counts* is that of the market. The higher the rating, the higher the price of the bond and the lower the

yield. As a point of interest, at the beginning of 1984, here is how the market rated the provinces:

1. Alberta, Ontario, Saskatchewan.
2. British Columbia, Manitoba.
3. Nova Scotia, New Brunswick.
4. Prince Edward Island.
5. Newfoundland.
6. Quebec.

The municipalities come next in the bond pecking order. They offer higher yields than the provinces, but I can't recommend them. In fact, I suggest you avoid all municipal issues. They lack marketability, and when there is a market the spread between the bid and the offer price is usually appalling. This means that whether you buy or sell in the after market, you will inevitably get shafted. The only justification for buying a municipal bond is to fulfill a civic obligation. If you have made a bundle in the big city and you want to help the folks back home in Squirrel's Ear pay for a new town hall, go ahead. But don't consider it an investment—consider it a donation.

Corporations are theoretically at the bottom of the credit pile. But some companies, such as Bell Telephone, have so high a credit rating that they can borrow at lower rates than most municipalities and many provinces. Corporations issue a variety of bonds. It is the cheapest way for them to raise capital because bond interest is paid *before taxes*, while dividends on preferred and common shares are paid *after taxes*. This is one reason why bond interest—regardless of the source—is *fully taxable* in your hands.

The senior security of a corporation is its first mortgage bonds. These are secured by a pledge on fixed assets. There are also second or General Mortgage bonds, which are secured by fixed assets, but rank *behind* the company's first mortgage bonds. A Collateral Trust bond is secured by a pledge of securities rather than fixed assets. A Debenture, is *not* secured by any pledge, other than the general credit of the issuer. Corporate bonds often have a feature known as a Sinking Fund. This may sound alarming, but in fact it is money set aside with a trustee (usually a trust company) which is used to buy back a percentage of the issue each year. This helps to support the price. Also, bonds can be Callable or Redeemable, which means they may be redeemed, in whole or in part, at the company's option. To compensate you for having your bond taken away, the call price contains a premium which declines with time. Thus, if your bonds are redeemed three years after issue the company might pay 102, but in the last few years before maturity the redemption price might be no more than par.

Occasionally a company will issue an Income bond or debenture. Income bonds only pay interest if the company can earn it. This should tell you that they carry a substantial element of risk. The good thing about income bonds is that the interest is treated for tax purposes the same as dividends and qualifies for the same tax credit. Another relatively rare type of bond is a Floating Rate debenture. This pays a rate of interest which is tied to the Prime Rate or some even more exotic financial index. Floating Rate debentures are designed to give the bondholder a measure of protection against an upward surge in interest rates. They are one of the innovations that the investment community has devised to sell bonds to a reluctant public. (During the past twenty years interest rates have trended steadily higher, and bonds have consequently been poor performers.) Another sales gimmick is to attach warrants or a similar "kicker" to a new bond issue. Warrants permit the holder to buy common shares of the company at a certain price for a fixed period of time. Warrants usually have a value—sometimes quite a substantial one—and as such are a bonus. They may be stripped from the bond and sold on the market, or exercised to buy the common stock at an advantageous price. You should only buy a bond with a kicker if you are confident that the company is financially sound *and* the outlook for the common shares is bright.

This also applies to Convertible bonds. A convertible bond is the most interesting, and potentially the most profitable bond of all. A convertible does not have warrants or any other kicker, but it may be *converted* into common shares of the company. The number of shares is determined at the time of issue and stated on the certificate. There are several advantages to owning a convertible bond. If the common shares go up, so will the bond, because it represents a given number of common shares. If interest rates drop, the bond will go up. Should the common shares fall and interest rates rise—the worst possible scenario—a convertible bond will perform better than a "straight" bond and show a smaller percentage loss than the underlying stock.

There are several things you must take into consideration before buying a convertible bond. First, do you like the underlying stock? If you are not bullish on the stock don't buy the bond. What about the conversion rate, and how long is it good for? It should be a realistic rate, and you should have at least four or five years left before maturity. Is the bond callable, and if so, when? This is *very* important, because if you are not careful you can buy a convertible at a big premium and then have it called at a much lower price. (In this case you would be forced to convert into the common shares because they would be worth more than the call price.) What about the yield on the bond, and how does it compare to the yield on the stock? The yield on a convertible will be less than a straight bond but it should be reasonable, and considerably more than the yield on the stock. If the yield on the stock and the bond are about the same, don't bother with the bond. Is the pay-back period two years or less? The pay-back period is the time it takes the bond to recoup the premium through its yield, compared with the yield on the stock. To explain this let us take a hypothetical example.

You are considering the purchase of a convertible bond at a price of 108. The bond yields eleven per cent and is callable at 104 in 1988. It is convertible into forty-five shares of common stock until 1990. The common stock is trading at twenty and the yield on it is two per cent at that price.

To figure out the *premium* multiply the number of shares by their price and deduct the total from the price of the bond:

45 shares × 20 = $900 – $1080 (the price of the bond) = $180
the $180 premium expressed as a percentage = 20%

To work out the *pay-back period* take the difference between the bond and the stock yields and divide it into the premium:

11% — 2% = 9% divided into 20% = 2.2 years

In this example the payback period was a little longer than ideal, but the bond is trading fairly close to its call price, and it has a good yield. You might buy it.

Convertible bonds can be very attractive investments. They are safer than common shares, but can appreciate at the same rate as the common. For this reason they are an ideal security for a Registered Retirement Savings Plan. In an RRSP both interest and capital gains are sheltered from tax. For aggressive investors convertible bonds can be margined at a lower rate than the common stock, and the interest on the bond helps to offset the interest charged on margin. Convertible bonds are also an excellent "hedge" against a short sale of the common. (Hedging will be explained later in the book.) For the average investor, convertibles are probably the best and safest way to make money in the bond market.

A new wrinkle in the bond market is the appearance of "zero coupon" bonds. Zero coupon bonds are derived from "high grade" issues (Canada or provincial bonds) that are separated from their coupons. The coupons and the principal amounts are then discounted and sold to investors. Zero coupon bonds do not pay anything until the maturity date, but the discounted price can provide a staggering *compounded* return. Take, for example, a stripped bond or a coupon maturing in twenty years and discount it at 12½ per cent. At this rate each dollar invested today would grow to $11.30 in twenty years. Because of the tax implications, zero coupon bonds are only suitable for non-taxable accounts. They also lack liquidity, so the average investor should only think of them as a Registered Retirement Savings Plan investment.

Recently, I noticed that a major trust company was advertising a new "money multiplier" called a Lion or a Tiger or some such name. Intrigued, I read the ad and saw that what was being offered with such fanfare were in fact zero coupon bonds. I was amused because my firm was offering the *same* Ontario Hydro zero coupons—without a fancy name—at a much better yield to investors. As I have said before, it pays to shop around.

When a new bond issue, or any other issue of securities is sold, an advertisement appears in the major newspapers. This advertisement gives the details of the issue, and the name of the underwriter or underwriters in order of precedence. Appropriately enough, it is known in the business as a "tombstone." By the time you see a tombstone in the paper, it is *too late to buy* the issue. (Unless it has been a failure, in which case you don't want it anyway.) On the following page is an illustration of a tombstone.

After a new issue is sold, the price fluctuates with supply and demand. When you buy or sell in the after market, you will be given a "subject" or a "firm" quote. A "subject" quote means "subject to confirmation" and the dealer is *not obligated* to do the trade. A "firm" quote means that the dealer is *committed* to trade at that price, for a specified period of time.

The confirmation or contract you receive from the broker when you buy or sell a bond is different than a stock confirma-

tion. Because the broker is acting as principal rather than agent in the transaction, the confirmation will say "sold to you" or "bought from you." It will also have an entry debiting or crediting you with *accrued interest*. This requires an explanation. When you buy a bond you are *charged* accrued interest from

the last day interest was paid on that bond. This is only fair, because the person who sold it would otherwise not receive his interest from that date, even though he was the beneficial owner of the bond. You will recoup the accrued interest when the next interest payment rolls around, thus the charge cancels itself out. When you sell a bond, you will be *credited* with accrued interest from the last payment date. If you sell bonds with coupons attached to them, be sure to detach *all* the coupons *except* for the current one. Here is an illustration of a bond confirmation:

You may be surprised to see that a commission charge is not shown on your confirmation. There is no commission on new issues, but when bonds are traded over the counter the dealer deducts from or adds to the price, depending upon whether he is buying the bonds from you or selling them to you. The amount he deducts or adds is his commission. As a rule the shorter the term of the bond, the smaller the charge. For example, the figure on Canada bonds maturing in three years might be ten cents or one dollar per thousand, while the charge on a long term bond could be fifty cents or five dollars per thousand. If you think you are being ripped-off, you can ask the broker what he is charging on the trade. The best protection against over-charging is to deal with a reputable firm, and with a broker you can trust.

Actually, commissions are a minor factor when trading bonds. Your main challenge is to correctly predict the direction of interest rates, and to catch the swings in the market. If you can do that, you will make money.

CHAPTER 6

Common Stocks

COMPARED TO BONDS, common stocks are a high risk investment. Indeed, there are all sorts of horror stories of people who have lost their shirts on common stocks. You may have heard some of them. On the other hand, when someone says he has made money in the market, the odds are fifty to one that he made it on this type of investment. It is also a fact that Canadian insurance companies hold hundreds of millions of dollars worth of common stocks in their portfolios. Obviously there's more to these shares than meets the eye.

Common stock represents the *equity* or *ownership* in a company. When you buy common shares of a company you become a part owner. As such you are exposed to both the rewards and the risks of ownership. If the business does well, your equity in the company and the value of your stock will increase. You will also participate in the earnings of the company. If the business does poorly, the reverse is true, your equity will shrink and your stock will decline in value. Should the company fail, you can lose your entire investment. (When a company goes bankrupt the common shareholders stand last in the line of creditors, after the bank, the bondholders, and the preferred shareholders.) I have a friend who built his dream house on the profits he made from common stocks. And I know another less fortunate fellow who ended up papering the wall of his bathroom with worthless common share certificates.

I have used "common stock" and "common shares" interchangeably, because they mean the same thing. Normally, each
share carries one vote in the election of the company's board of
directors. Thus the common shareholders have a voice in the
management of the company. Also, at the discretion of the board
of directors, they may receive payments each quarter in the
form of *dividends* on their stock. Unlike bond interest, which is
at a *fixed rate*, there is no set rate for common dividends. Dividends on the common shares are paid *after all expenses* (including bond interest and dividends on preferred shares) and are
not cumulative. This means that if a quarterly dividend is skipped
there is no obligation for the company to pay it later. That's the
bad news about dividends. The good news is that dividends of
Canadian companies qualify for a special tax credit—unlike bond
interest or any other form of interest.

There are two reasons for the tax credit. The first is that the
company has already paid tax on the money before paying it to
you; the second is that the government wants to encourage
Canadian ownership. The tax credit works in this way. Your dividend is "grossed-up" (overstated) by fifty per cent on the T-5
which you receive from the company, or from your broker if he
holds the shares. You are then allowed to deduct thirty-four per
cent of the *actual* dividend from Federal Tax payable on your
Taxable Income. Supposing you receive $1000 in dividends dur-
ing the year. The calculation would look like this:

> Actual dividend $1000
> 50% gross-up   + $ 500
> Total Reported $1500
> 34% of actual dividend = $340
> Therefore, $340 may be deducted from Federal Tax Payable.

The foregoing may look complicated, but as both the actual
and the grossed-up figures are printed on your T-5 it is relatively
straightforward. If you want to compare dividend income and
interest income, just multiply the dividend by 1.5 to get an
approximate equivalent. For instance a dividend of six per cent
is roughly equal to nine per cent interest, after tax.

I don't want to dwell on dividends, because many common stocks pay little or no dividend, including stocks of some first rate companies. Nevertheless, you should know about dividends. The main reason for buying common stocks is to get a piece of the action—capital gain. This makes good sense. Studies show that over the years common stocks have vastly outperformed fixed income securities as a hedge against inflation.

Common stocks range from "blue chips" to "penny dreadfuls." (A "blue chip" is a seasoned company with a strong balance sheet, while a "penny dreadful" is a speculative stock whose main asset is hope.) But before discussing the various types of common stocks I'd like to touch on some more of the basics. One point that should be cleared up concerns the capitalization of a business. Many people believe that if the shares of company "A" are selling at ten dollars, and the shares of company "B" are trading at twenty, the stock of company "A" is twice as good a buy as company "B." Even if we assume that both companies have the same prospects, and the same net worth, the twenty dollar stock could in fact offer better value than the ten dollar stock. It all depends on the capitalization of the two companies.

Think of two identical pies. One pie is cut into six pieces, the other into fourteen pieces. Now substitute "company" for "pie" and substitute "shares" for "pieces." Shares represent pieces of the corporate pie, and a key factor is how big or how small are the pieces of the pie. For example if company "A" had one million shares, and company "B" had only one hundred thousand, then the shares of company "B" would be worth *theoretically* ten times as much as the other company. (Because the pieces of the "pie" are ten times as big.) Assuming that both companies have a net worth of one million dollars, here is the calculation:

$1,000,000 divided by 1,000,000 shares = $1
$1,000,000 divided by 100,000 shares = $10

It might be mentioned that there are *two* figures to watch for when checking the number of shares of a company. One is the amount of Authorized shares, the other the number of Issued shares. The authorized amount is the total number that the company is allowed to issue under its corporate charter, the issued amount is the number that are actually outstanding. Of the two, the *issued* number is the one that counts. Also, common shares either have a Par Value expressed in dollars, or No Par Value. The par value of a common share is its stated face value as assigned by the company's charter. It bears no relationship to the *market value*, and is so irrelevant that most companies now only issue no par value (NPV) common stock.

When I was a boy, I found a sheaf of mining certificates that had belonged to my grandfather. Many of the certificates were engraved with the words "Par Value One Dollar" and a quick count showed that at least fifty thousand shares bore these magic words. Astounded at the bonanza I had stumbled upon, I rushed to my father with the certificates. Dad riffled through them, and to my chagrin told me they were worthless. It was then that I learned what par value means to common shares—nothing. It does, however, have considerable significance to preferred shares, which will be discussed in the next chapter.

The yield of a stock is the annual dividend expressed as a percentage of the current price of the shares. It is easy to calculate by simply dividing the price of the stock into its dividend. Thus if a stock pays $1.50 per year and is trading at thirty dollars the dividend yield is five per cent.

This is the way a stock quotation appears in the newspaper:

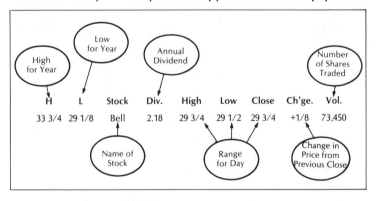

How do you value a stock? Both the number of shares outstanding and their yield (if any) should be considered, but this is only the tip of the iceberg. The next thing to find out is the earnings per share. This is done by dividing the number of common shares into the company's net earnings. (Net earnings or net profit is what's left over after all taxes and expenses have been paid.) If a company had one million shares outstanding and its net earnings were two million dollars, the earnings per share would be two dollars.

Having established the earnings per share, you are now in position to make a most important calculation—the relationship between the price of the stock and its earnings per share. This is known as the P/E or Price/Earnings ratio. To find this ratio you divide the per share earnings into the price of the stock. This will give you the Price/Earnings ratio. Let us take the foregoing example of two dollars. By dividing two (the earnings) into thirty (the share price) you come up with a figure of fifteen. Therefore the stock is trading at a price equal to fifteen times its annual earnings, and has a Price/Earnings ratio of 15:1.

The Price/Earnings ratio is a popular yardstick to measure whether a stock is overvalued or undervalued, and it is also used to compare stocks within a given industry. The *Monthly Review* published by the Toronto Stock Exchange (which you can obtain from your broker) lists the various industries, and their average Price/Earnings ratios.

Broadly speaking, common shares can be divided into two categories—growth stocks and income stocks. Growth stocks yield less than income stocks, and trade at a higher Price/Earnings ratio. For instance, at the beginning of 1984 Northern Telecom was selling at twenty times earnings while B.C. Telephone was selling at nine times earnings. The reason for this price difference was that the earnings of Northern Telecom were increasing at a much faster rate than those of B.C. Telephone. The market always *discounts future earnings,* and investors normally pay a *premium* for superior performance. In the case of Northern Telecom and B.C. Telephone, on the following page are the earnings per share for the previous two years.

	Earnings Per Share		
	1982	1983	Increase
B.C. Telephone	$2.11	$2.36	12%
Northern Telecom	$1.26	$2.05	63%

Within the two broad categories—growth stocks and income stocks—there are a number of sub groups. Before discussing them, let's look at the grading system that applies to all stocks. At the top of the list we have the "blue chips" which, as I mentioned, are proven companies with strong balance sheets and a consistent earnings record. Among the blue chip companies are names like Canadian Pacific, Bell Canada, Imperial Oil, and the major chartered banks. (Inco was once the most famous Canadian blue chip of all, but Inco has fallen upon hard times and is now more of a brown chip.) The next level, where a great many good stocks are found, has smaller companies or companies with less impressive earnings records. The third tier contains stocks that are often classed as "businessman's risk" situations. The term "businessman's risk" is an industry euphemism which spares the broker the need to tell his client: "If this one bombs, no crying towel is provided." Dome Petroleum is described by most brokers as a businessman's risk. Other brokers place Dome Pete at the bottom of the heap where the weak and the terminally ill companies reside, along with the penny dreadfuls.

Growth stocks can be divided into *senior* companies and *emerging* ones. The emerging companies are the most sensational performers—and the most susceptible to disaster. Mitel, the Ottawa based "high tech" company, is typical of this category. Mitel first issued common stock to the public in 1979 at ten dollars per share. During the following year the stock was split three-for-one and the value of the original shares soared to nearly $150. Since then Mitel has suffered reverses and the stock has come down a long way, but the shares are still well above the original issue price.

Emerging growth stocks rarely pay a dividend because the earnings are ploughed back into the business, and they often sell at an astronomical Price/Earnings ratio. They are not for widows and orphans, but if you can afford the risk, you can sometimes make a lot of money on them.

Leading companies in strong industries are considered to be senior growth stocks. Northern Telecom is a good example. This type of stock pays a relatively small dividend and trades at an above average Price/Earnings ratio. If income is not a prime consideration, a senior growth stock is an excellent inflation hedge. It should be mentioned, however, that when the market goes into a prolonged slump, as it did in 1981 and 1982, both the emerging *and* the senior growth stocks take a pounding. This phenomenon is not restricted to growth stocks; in a bear market most senior issues are caught in the downdraft.

Companies in cyclical industries are not strictly speaking growth stocks, but if you buy them at the right time they can produce big capital gains. Cyclical industries are ones that are particularly sensitive to the economy or to a change in commodity prices. This includes the auto makers, mining companies, cement producers, steel companies, and the forest products industry. For instance, when the economy enters a recession the amount of advertising in newspapers drops sharply. As a result the pulp and paper companies sell much less newsprint, which hurts their earnings. When the economy picks up, so does the demand for newsprint. Eventually, the earnings of the pulp and paper companies recover, as do the prices of their shares. This produces a roller coaster ride for investors.

Debt leverage is another factor that contributes to wide swings in the earnings of many cyclical companies. If a company has a lot of debt (bonds) in relation to its equity (common shares) this means a heavy fixed charge on earnings. During bad times there is little or nothing left over for the common shareholders, but in good times the earnings of the common can increase dramatically. For example, let us assume that a company must earn $800,000 to service the annual interest on its debt. If it earns $1,000,000, there will be $200,000 left over (before tax) for the common shareholders. Now let's see what happens if the company suffers a twenty per cent *decline* in its earnings:

Company earnings	$800,000
Cost to service debt	– $800,000
Amount available for common	nil

That's the harsh side of debt leverage, now here is the good side. Let us assume that the company has a twenty per cent *increase* in earnings. Look what it does for the common shareholders:

Company earnings	$1,200,000
Cost to service debt	– $ 800,000
Amount available for common	$400,000

In this example a twenty per cent increase in the company's earnings has raised the pre-tax amount available for the common by one hundred per cent.

Astute investors watch cyclical stocks closely. The trick is to buy them when the industry is in the doldrums, and to ride them up with the recovery. If a cyclical company is highly leveraged so much the better, you will get an even bigger lift. Being cyclical, these stocks inevitably reach a crest—usually near the end of the economic boom—and then go into a long descent. So the *timing of your sale* is every bit as important as the timing of your purchase.

Alcan Aluminum is the best quality cyclical stock in Canada, and for all practical purposes qualifies as a blue chip. The three major steel companies (Dofasco, Algoma and Stelco) are also first rate cyclical stocks. If you want a "double play" watch Noranda, because Noranda not only owns copper, gold, and other mines, but it is also the largest forest products producer in the country.

In the transition zone between growth stocks and income stocks there are three groups to consider. One consists of mature companies that pay a reasonable dividend and at the same time offer reasonable growth. Canadian Pacific, Moore Corporation, and Royal Trust are typical of this category. Then there are the "defensive stocks" which offer essential services, or products that are not affected by a recession. This type of company can also pass on price increases to its customers. Food stores, brewers, and utilities fall into this group. During a recession people must eat, they will continue to drink (the cheapest alcoholic beverage), and they must have light and heat. Some of the names that come to mind are Dominion Stores, Loblaw, Labatt, Molson, Consumers' Gas, and TransAlta Utilities. The third group consists of the banks.

Canada's chartered banks have an enviable reputation for strength and stability. In 1983, forty-eight banks in the United States folded, but there hasn't been a bank failure in Canada since 1926. I am frequently critical of the banks, but I certainly like them as an investment. A chartered bank occupies the same position in the economy as the croupier in a casino—you or I may win or lose, but they win every time. The chartered banks sell at low Price/Earnings ratios and offer generous yields, as well as *excellent* growth. I think every portfolio should contain some bank stock. The only cloud on the banks' horizon is the huge amount of money they have lent to underdeveloped countries. If all the countries defaulted, the banks would be in dire straits. (However, I suspect that if this happened, the Canadian Government would intervene.) In recent years there has been a proliferation of chartered banks in Canada. If you are a novice investor my advice would be to restrict your purchases to the shares of the Big Five. They are, in alphabetical order:

Bank of Montreal
Bank of Nova Scotia
Canadian Imperial Bank of Commerce
Royal Bank
Toronto-Dominion Bank

In the past few years both the Royal Bank and the Toronto-Dominion have split their stock. A stock split means that the shares you hold are subdivided into smaller units. For instance, if the split is on a three-for-one basis, each one of your "old" shares will become three "new" shares. As a result of the split the shares will *drop* in price because the theoretical value of the new shares is one third of the old. (Remember it's still the same size pie, but the pieces are now smaller.) The main reason for a stock split is to bring the cost of the shares down to a popular price level—say ten to twenty dollars—and thereby make them more attractive to investors. A second reason is to improve the marketability of the stock by increasing the number of shares outstanding. Investors like stock splits because it usually results in an immediate gain on the total value of their holding.

From time to time the chartered banks also issue rights. A "right" permits the shareholder to purchase stock at what is essentially a discount price. Normally the shareholder receives one right for each share. Rights may be exercised or sold—either way they are a benefit to the shareholder, and increase the return on the stock. The purchase formula varies, but involves one or more rights plus cash to buy one additional share. For instance, if the shares of a company are trading at twenty dollars, it might take five rights plus eighteen dollars to subscribe for one new share. This would give each right a theoretical value of forty cents. Here is the calculation:

$$5 \text{ rights} + \$18 = \$20 \text{ (one share)}$$
$$5 \text{ rights} = \$20 - \$18$$
$$5 \text{ rights} = \$2$$
$$1 \text{ right} = \underline{.40}$$

The reason a company issues rights is to raise additional equity capital. The logic behind giving rights to the existing shareholders is that it allows them, if they wish, to maintain their percentage of stock in the company. After a rights issue is announced the stock trades *cum rights* for a short period of time. Anyone who buys the shares during the *cum rights* period receives the rights. By the same token, if you sell your shares before the stock goes *ex rights* you will *not* receive the rights. There is always an active market in rights, so it is easy to buy more (if you want to add to your holding) or to sell all or part of your rights. Rights are usually only valid for a period of weeks, after which they become *worthless*. Therefore you must act *promptly* when you receive rights. I've often had clients come in with a sheepish look and say that they forgot to exercise or sell their rights. If you do that, it's the same as throwing away money.

In the investment sense a "warrant" can mean one of two things. It is either a *certificate* for rights or a *long term* right to buy shares. Because warrants provide a long term call on the stock, they have a time value in addition to their intrinsic value. For instance, Alcan warrants permit the holder to buy one common share at $36.50 until 31 December 1986. At the end of 1983, when Alcan was trading at $49.50, this warrant had an *intrinsic* value of $13.00 but was selling at $20.75 or a premium of nearly sixty per cent. The premium was the time value. As the time runs out on the life of a warrant, the premium *declines* to the intrinsic value. The way you calculate the intrinsic value of a warrant is to deduct the exercise price from the current price of the stock. At the close of 1983, these were the figures on Alcan:

Price of Alcan common share	$49.50
Exercise price of warrant	− $36.50
Intrinsic value of warrant	$13.00

Both warrants and rights are leveraged investments because a small price change in the underlying stock can make a huge percentage change in their value. This gives them speculative appeal. They are also an attractive way to play expensive stocks with a small cash outlay. But don't forget, eventually they expire and when this happens, it's game over.

The classic income stocks—those of the telephone, power, and gas utilities—also issue rights on a fairly regular basis. For investors, this increases the effective yield on these stocks. Some of the companies in this category are Maritime Electric, Gaz Metropolitan, Newfoundland Light and Power, and, of course, Bell Enterprises Limited.

These companies are considered to have limited growth potential because they operate monopolies. As a result of this situation, governments regulate what they may charge for their services. This means that their earnings grow quite slowly and frequently lag behind the pace of inflation. However, because they can predict their earnings with reasonable certainty, they can safely pay out a high percentage in dividends. Another factor is that these companies *never* have a problem with accounts receivable. If you don't pay your gas or telephone bill the service will be disconnected—and you can't switch to another company. This acts as a powerful incentive to pay your account on time.

Investors looking for growth usually ignore the utility stocks. I don't, and would urge you to consider them carefully. As I mentioned they pay generous dividends, and over the years these dividends steadily increase. You can't say that for a bond. In fact, for my widows and orphans I often recommend Bell stock in lieu of regular bonds. Bell is sensitive to interest rates (the same as a bond) but it has an element of growth, and the dividend has a tax credit. In 1983 Bell spun-off its non-regulated holdings, which include a controlling interest in Northern Telecom. This will permit Bell to earn whatever the traffic will bear on a significant portion of its assets, and enhance its growth prospects. It was also in 1983 that Bell increased its dividend by twenty-two cents per share. In 1984 Bell bought control of TransCanada Pipelines, a major utility that transports natural gas from the prairie provinces to Eastern Canada. During 1983 the price of Bell common rose from $24\frac{3}{8}$ to $33\frac{1}{2}$ for a gain of nearly forty per cent. Not bad for a widow and orphan's stock!

I should also add that most of the utility companies have dividend reinvestment programs. This means that you can choose *not* to receive your dividends in cash, but to have the proceeds used to buy more shares. As a broker it pains me to tell you this, but the shares will be bought at a reduced commission and you may even buy them at a discount. TransAlta, for instance, has a dividend reinvestment program that buys shares at a discount of five per cent from the average market price. No broker—even a discount house—can match this deal.

The only time a broker can sell you shares at a discount from the market price is when there is a Secondary Offering. This type of transaction occurs when a block of stock comes up for sale that is too large to be absorbed in regular trading. To facilitate the sale of the block, the shares are discounted by a small amount and sold at a net price. Often there is little warning before a Secondary Offering is made, as this tends to depress the price. When an offering takes place on the floor of the exchange, it must be completed in a short period of time. Because speed is essential, when your broker phones he will press you for a quick decision.

Unless you are already considering the purchase of the stock, you should pass up a Secondary Offering. The discount is *not* a sufficient reason to buy, and the seller may be unloading the shares because he considers them overvalued. Even if there is a legitimate reason for the secondary, once it has been completed the shares will probably decline in price. This is not surprising if you think about it—the secondary will have sopped up all the buying interest. Normally, I don't even bother to call my clients when there is a Secondary Offering.

If you are a serious investor, you cannot afford to ignore the American stock market. In Canada, a high percentage of our stocks are resource oriented, and even the supply of these companies is dwindling as a result of amalgamations and takeovers. The U.S. market is much broader based, and offers an incredible array of investment choices. To give you an idea of the variety, here are some of the common stocks listed on the New York Stock Exchange:

American Express	Ford	Playboy
American Motors	General Electric	Polaroid
Avon	General Motors	Quaker Oats
Bausch & Lomb	Gillette	RCA
Black & Decker	Heinz	Ralston Purina
Boeing	IBM	Revlon
Borden	Kellogg	Rubbermaid
Cessna	Eli Lilly	Smucker's
Champion Spark Plug	Lockheed	Sony
Chrysler	Macy's	Squibb
Coca-Cola	Maytag	Telex
Coleco	Merrill Lynch	Uniroyal
Colgate-Palmolive	Nabisco	Wells Fargo
Dart & Kraft	Outboard Marine	Wrigley
Delta Airlines	PanAm	Xerox
Eastman Kodak	Pepsi Cola	Zenith
Fabergé	Pitney Bowes	

The two main exchanges in the United States are the New York Stock Exchange and the American Stock Exchange. The senior one is the New York Stock Exchange, which also has the lion's share of important listings.

I like U.S. stocks for a number of reasons. They are more volatile than Canadian stocks, so if you are right in your choice you don't have to wait long for a stock to move. The markets are also highly liquid, which means that you can get in or *out* of a stock in a hurry, and you can trade in quantity. There is another less obvious reason for owning U.S. shares, and that is the currency hedge they provide. I think it is prudent to have some of your assets in American dollars. Dividends from U.S. stocks are also useful, particularly if you travel or vacation in the States.

For Canadians, there are two principal drawbacks to U.S. stocks. First, dividends are subject to an automatic withholding tax of fifteen per cent. This tax is deducted at source, so your dividend is reduced by that amount. You do *not* receive any special tax credit on U.S. dividends from Revenue Canada, but you are allowed to claim the amount of the withholding tax on your Canadian income tax return. Secondly, if you have U.S. shares registered in your name when you die, your estate may be subject to succession duties from the states in which the companies are domiciled. To avoid this problem, leave your U.S. stocks with your broker (registered in the firm's name), or have them registered in the name of a bank or a trust company.

If you plan to trade American stocks I would recommend that you open a U.S. funds account with your broker. This will eliminate the need to convert from Canadian to American dollars (or vice versa) every time you do a transaction. I might mention that you will normally get a better rate from your broker than from your bank when converting U.S. or Canadian funds. The broker will take less on the exchange transaction to facilitate the trade—which is where he makes his money. It goes without saying that a Canadian broker who is a member of the New York and American Exchanges will give you better service than one who is not.

The only other word of warning is to stay away from American unlisted stocks. This also applies, but to a lesser degree, to stocks that trade on NASDAQ, which is the acronym for National Association of Securities Dealers Automated Quotations, a computerized over-the-counter facility. With the choice of stocks available to you on U.S. exchanges, there is no conceivable reason to play in the unlisted market.

The same advice goes for the Canadian unlisted market. There are enough good common stocks on the Canadian exchanges to keep you profitably occupied for the rest of your life.

CHAPTER 7

Preferred Shares

PREFERRED SHARES ARE primarily an income investment. They are also a hybrid security in that they have some of the characteristics of both bonds and common shares. To compensate for the fact that preferred shares do *not* participate in a company's growth, they pay a larger dividend than its common stock. Because preferred dividends are paid from after tax earnings, they qualify for the dividend tax credit. This combination—a high dividend rate with a tax credit—can provide dramatic returns.

The tax credit on Canadian preferred dividends is the same as for dividends on common shares. When you make your return the dividends are "grossed-up" by fifty per cent, then thirty-four per cent of the *actual* amount you received is deducted from Federal Tax. If your income consists solely of dividends from Canadian companies, an astounding amount will be tax free. In 1983 for example, an Ontario resident who was single with no dependents could have had dividend income totalling $39,500 and not paid one cent of tax!

I should warn you, before launching into a dissertation on preferred shares, that it's a heavy subject. If you are only interested in the fast track, I suggest you skip this chapter and move on to the next. On the other hand, if you want a working knowledge of a useful investment, stick with me. Once we get through this part of the labyrinth, the path will be clearer.

Like common shares, preferred shares are part of the equity of a company. But they are a safer investment. They get their name because they have preference over the common on both the earnings and the assets of the company. In the event of dissolution, preferred shares rank behind the bank and the bondholders but ahead of the common shareholders. When dividends are declared, the preferred shares have first call on the earnings. Preferred shares usually do *not* have a vote, unless dividend payments are in arrears.

Normally the dividend on a preferred share is set at a fixed rate like the coupon on a bond, and it does not change even if the company's earnings increase. A preferred share is also similar to a bond in that it has a par value. The par value is *its stated value*, and is important for two reasons.

First, the par value is a claim on the assets of the company to that amount, and must be satisfied before anything is paid to the common shareholders. Therefore a preferred share with a par value of twenty-five dollars is entitled to twenty-five dollars in the event of dissolution or winding up of the company.

Secondly, the dividend is often expressed as a percentage of the par value. For instance, a twenty-five dollar par preferred share paying a $2.00 dividend (which is 8%) may be described as a $2.00 preferred or an eight per cent preferred. Both descriptions are correct—it depends upon the issuer as to which form is used.

From the company's point of view, preferred shares are the most expensive way to raise capital. This is due to the fact dividends are paid from earnings *after* all taxes. Why do companies issue preferred shares? Usually it is to increase their equity base, or because their credit is so weak that they can't sell bonds. (In the latter case brokers don't use those words, but say "the market is not receptive to a debt issue at this time.")

This leads us to two ratios you should scrutinize before you buy a preferred share; the *asset coverage* and the *dividend coverage*. The figures for both ratios should be the *average* over the previous *five* years.

To determine the asset coverage look at the company's balance sheet and note the "Total Shareholders' Equity." This section will show the common shares outstanding as well as any preferred share issues. Simply divide the number of preferred shares into "Total Shareholders' Equity." The figure you come up with is the asset coverage per preferred share. For example, suppose you were considering the purchase of a preferred that was the only one outstanding. Here is how you would calculate the asset coverage:

Total Shareholders' Equity	$9,500,000
200,000 8% preferred $10 par shares	
$9,500,000 ÷ 200,000	= 47.50
Asset coverage per preferred share	= $47.50
Expressed as a ratio it is 4.75:1 or 4.75 times	

Now if this same company was to issue more shares, say 200,000 six per cent preferred with a par value of fifteen dollars, which ranked *junior* to the eight per cent preferred, this is how you would figure out the asset coverage on the new issue:

Total Shareholders' Equity	$9,500,000
Less 200,000 8% preferred $10 par	− $2,000,000
Balance available to new preferred	$7,500,000
Divide $7,500,000 by 200,000	= 37.50
Asset coverage per new preferred	= $37.50
Expressed as a ratio it is 2.5:1 or 2.5 times	

The asset coverage is critical because it represents the cushion of equity in the event of liquidation. As a rule of thumb, the *minimum* asset coverage for utility shares should be 2:1 and for corporate preferred shares 3:1.

The Dividend Coverage is also very important. It can be calculated by a complicated formula or by a simple one. I prefer the simple way, which is to divide the total preferred dividend requirement into the total *net earnings* (excluding extraordinary items). Sometimes there are one or more preferreds which rank *pari passu* (a Latin phrase meaning "equally"); in this case make a lump sum of the total dividend requirement and divide it into the net earnings. Here are two examples:

Company net earnings	$800,000
200,000 8% preferred $10 par	
Dividend requirement (200,000 × .80)	= $160,000
Divide requirement into earnings	= 5
Divide coverage	= 5:1

Going back to the second Asset Coverage example, let us assume that you want to find out the dividend coverage on the six per cent preferred which is *junior* to the eight per cent preferred:

Company net earnings	$800,000
Less 8% preferred dividend	− $160,000
Balance available for 6% preferred	$640,000
Dividend requirement (200,000 × .90)	= $180,000
Divide requirement into earnings	= 3.5
Dividend Coverage	= 3.5:1 or 3.5 times

The *earnings trend* is another factor to take into consideration when calculating dividend coverage. If the earnings are *erratic* or if there is a *downward* trend, this is a bad sign. You can spot the earnings trend by comparing the common share earnings for the past five years. Here is an example of a solid earnings trend:

Common Share Earnings

1984	1983	1982	1981	1980	1979
$3.59	$2.86	$2.38	$2.24	$2.01	$1.77

The *minimum* acceptable coverage for utility shares is two times the dividend requirement, and for corporate preferreds it is three times the dividend requirement. I would suggest that you avoid preferred shares that do not measure up to these minimum standards.

For those of you who don't want to punch a calculator, the rating services maintain credit ratings on most of the actively traded preferred shares. Preferreds designated "P2" by Canadian Bond Rating Service or "BBB" by Dominion Bond Rating Service would be the *minimum* ratings you should consider.

Aside from the credit rating of a preferred share, there are a couple of legal features you must check. One concerns the dividend and whether it is *cumulative* or *non-cumulative*. A cumulative dividend means that if a quarterly dividend is passed, it remains an obligation on the books of the company. Sometimes a company will get into financial difficulty and pass its preferred dividends for several years and then, after it recovers, pay them in one lump. If, however, the shares are non-cumulative and a dividend is passed, you are out of luck. Thus, it is prudent to only buy *cumulative* preferred shares.

The other thing to watch out for is the "call" feature. Many preferred shares may be *redeemed* by the company on or after a set date, at a fixed price. Usually, the company will pay more than the par value on the call date, but the price declines in each succeeding year to par. The reason for the premium price at the outset is to compensate the holder for the loss of his shares. If the shares are called some time after the redemption date, it is assumed that the holder will suffer less pain at giving up his stock. Some preferred shares are non-callable or non-redeemable, but this is becoming increasingly rare.

If you pay a price significantly above par for a redeemable preferred, you run the risk of losing money if your shares are called. (This does not apply to convertible preferreds that are trading at a premium due to the underlying common stock.) The hazard is particularly great with some of the big coupon preferreds that were issued during the last bout of high interest rates. The closer the call date, the greater the potential for loss. The further away the call date, the longer you have to write-off the premium. The time element is reflected in the prices investors are willing to pay for redeemable preferreds. In March 1984, Brascan "A" Preferred, which was callable in twenty-six months, was only trading at a premium of one dollar over the call price. At the same time, B.C. Telephone's 11.24% Preferred, which had more than eight years to run before the redemption date, was selling at a premium of more than four dollars over the call price.

Before leaving the topic I should also mention that a company is *not* compelled to redeem its shares, it merely has the right to do so. Nonetheless, when assessing a preferred you should *assume that it will be called on the redemption date*. This way you won't be in for an unpleasant surprise. The best solution, if you can manage it, is to buy redeemable preferreds at issue price. Or stick to non-redeemable preferreds.

For many years there was only one kind of preferred share, the "straight preferred." This is akin to a perpetual bond in that it has no fixed term, except in cases where there is a redemption feature. Aside from being called, the only way these shares are removed from circulation is through open market purchases by the company. This is done on a limited scale by the company's purchase or sinking fund. Because straight preferreds are similar to a bond, they respond to interest rates the same as any other fixed income security. When interest rates rise, preferreds fall, and vice versa. As interest rates have been in an upward trend for the past twenty years, the performance of straight preferreds has been dismal. Today, there are only half a dozen issues that are readily marketable.

Straight preferreds are a pure interest rate play, and a poor one at that. I would suggest that you avoid *all* straight preferred shares, *regardless* of the yield. None of my clients own straight preferreds because I weed them out as soon as I come upon them. If you own any straight preferred shares, my recommendation is to sell them and take your loss.

As a digression, investors sometimes confuse Class "A" and Class "B" common shares with straight preferred shares. Whether they are Class A or B, (or Class X or Y) common shares participate in the earnings of the company. However, Class A shares are usually *not* entitled to a vote, but have a preference on the dividend. After the Class A shares have been paid a given amount, the Class B shares are paid a like amount, then *both* classes share equally in any further dividend payments. For example, Molson's has Class A and Class B common shares outstanding. The Class A shares have no vote but are entitled to a dividend of twenty cents before anything is paid to the Class B shares.

When there are two classes of common shares, you should normally buy the ones that carry a vote, because this can make your stock more valuable in the event of a takeover offer. But this is *not* a hard and fast rule. Each company is different and must be assessed on its own merits. In the case of Molson's common, the A shares trade at a *premium* to the B because the A shares are more marketable. This paradox is true of several major companies with non-voting common shares.

Speaking of common stock leads us to another type of preferred, Convertible Preferred shares. They are more volatile than straight preferreds, and have a much greater profit potential. Convertible preferred shares are both an income and an equity investment because they can be exchanged into common shares of the company. Conversion terms vary with each issue, but the effect is to lock in a set price on the common for a given period of time. Thus, if the underlying common shares rise, or if interest rates fall, the preferred will increase in value. On the other hand, if the common shares decline the convertible preferred will be protected to some extent by the yield on its dividend.

Although they offer the best of both worlds, convertible preferreds must be selected with care. The first thing to ask yourself is whether you want to own the common stock. If you don't like the common, forget the convertible preferred. Convertible preferreds pay a *lower* dividend rate than other preferreds, and when they are issued the conversion rate is always *above* the current price of the common. The difference between the conversion rate and the current price of the common stock is known as the "time premium" or "premium." For instance, a convertible preferred might be issued at twenty-five dollars (its par value) and be convertible share for share into the common or a period of six years. If the common is trading at twenty dollars, then the conversion premium is five dollars or twenty-five per cent. Depending upon the yield of the preferred *and* the outlook for the common stock, this may or may not be an attractive investment.

The premium on a convertible preferred is also influenced by a number of other factors. The *payback period* is a major consideration. This is the time it will take for the additional yield on the preferred to pay for the premium, or excess amount, above the current conversion price of the common. If the premium is twenty-five per cent and the difference in yield between the preferred and the common is five per cent, the payback period would be five years. Here is the calculation:

Preferred yield   8%
Common yield   − 3%
Additional yield on the preferred = 5%
Divide yield difference of 5% into premium of 25%
Payback period = 5 (years)

To show the importance of the *payback period* in valuing the premium on a convertible preferred, here is a recent comparison of two listed issues:

	Price			Yield		Payback
Name	Pfd	Common	Premium	Pfd	Common	Period
Bell $2.70	33⅜	30¼	11.2%	8.0	7.2	14 years
Bow Valley $2.00	34¾	25⅝	16.6%	5.9	0.6	3 years

At first glance, Bell would appear to be better value because it has a higher yield and a lower premium. But it is *not*. There is so little difference between the yield on Bell common and its $2.70 convertible preferred that it would take fourteen years to recoup the premium. You would be better off to buy Bell common stock. Bow Valley pays a small dividend on its common, which accounts for the short payback period on the convertible preferred. Investors who want greater income and safety, but are bullish on Bow Valley common, would be justified in buying the convertible preferred.

You must also watch the *call* feature on convertible preferreds. If you pay a big premium for a convertible with less than three years to its call date, you could be in trouble. Should the shares be called, you will be given a month or so to convert, which is fine providing the common has risen enough to recoup your premium. If not, you are faced with a sure loss. To minimize the amount of your loss choose whichever is higher, the redemption price of the preferred *or* the converted value of the common.

This also applies to the *expiry date* of the conversion privilege, if there is one. Some convertible preferreds revert to being straight preferreds after a specified period of time. Others have an escalating scale on the conversion privilege, whereby exercising into the common becomes more expensive after a certain date. Before you buy a convertible preferred make sure you are familiar with the terms of the issue, and, if necessary, read a copy of the original prospectus. Your broker can obtain one for you.

I seem to have stressed the negative aspects of convertible preferreds, when in fact they are usually excellent investments. Indeed, even the Bell $2.70 preferred which I mentioned earlier has been a winner. It was issued at twenty dollars and has not only paid a whacking big dividend, but has appreciated by more than fifty per cent in the last two years. Others have done even better.

By 1978 rising interest rates had destroyed the market for new issues of straight preferreds. In response to the problem underwriters came up with two new versions of the straight preferred. One was the Variable Rate Preferred, the other the Retractable Preferred. Both have been successful, and since then billions of dollars of these issues have been bought by Canadian investors.

A Variable Rate Preferred is the same as a straight preferred with one important exception—the total dividend is *not* fixed, but is tied to prevailing interest rates. If interest rates rise, so will the dividends. Normally, there is a fixed *minimum dividend* that will be paid even if interest rates decline. Thus shareholders can count on a certain minimum level of income, and they will also participate if interest rates move up. There is no set formula for the variable rate, each preferred of this type is different from the other.

Recently the Bank of Montreal issued a variable rate preferred which is cumulative and redeemable with a par value of twenty-five dollars. The minimum dividend is $2.125 or 8½% on the par value. The variable rate will commence on 26 February 1989 which is five years *after* the date of issue. Here is the variable rate formula: The greater of the fixed dividend, or seventy-five per cent of the average of the Prime Rate of the Bank during the first month of the quarter preceding the dividend payment date.

The formula sounds complicated, but basically it means that the dividend rate each quarter will be three quarters of the Bank of Montreal's Prime Rate. If the Prime averages 12% the quarterly dividend will rise to 9%, but if the Prime is only 8% the minimum dividend of 8½% will prevail.

I advised my clients not to buy this issue for two reasons. The first is the wait of five years before the variable rate comes into play. The second is the fact that the issue can be called by the bank on 1 February 1989. Conceivably, after receiving the minimum dividend for five years, you could lose your shares just three weeks before the variable rate begins. Stranger things have happened.

Ideally, a variable rate preferred should have a generous minimum dividend, and a waiting period of not more than one year before the variable rate commences. It should also measure up to all the other investment standards of a good preferred. I find it difficult to get enthusiastic about variable rate preferreds—to my mind Retractable Preferreds are a more attractive investment.

A retractable preferred is also similar to a straight preferred, but is has an escape feature—the holder has the right to sell it back to the company *at issue price* on a future date. This makes a retractable preferred something like a dividend paying bond because of the assured return of capital and the fixed rate of income. Unlike a bond, however, the dividend has the tax credit.

Retractable preferreds have been very popular with investors. At the end of 1983, there were more than seventy of these issues outstanding. Many retractables are now trading at substantial premiums above their original issue price. For this reason you can't buy them simply on a yield basis, you *must* check the quality and terms of each issue.

Virtually all the retractable preferreds have a call feature. This means that you have *three yields* to consider: current yield, yield to retraction, and yield to redemption. The real ones, and the ones that count, are yield to *retraction* and yield to *redemption*. Here is an example to show how you can be fooled if you just look at the current yield. Both of these preferreds are retractable and redeemable in 1986:

Security	Price	Dividend	Current Yield	Retraction Yield	Redemption Yield
Alberta Energy	31¼	$3.75	12.00%	5.06%	6.77%
Brascan A Pfd.	27¼	$2.69	9.86%	6.40%	8.33%

As this shows, although Alberta Energy has a much higher current yield, its *true* yield—to redemption or retraction—is lower than that of Brascan.

If you buy a retractable with a big premium you will inevitably suffer a loss. Even if interest rates remain stable. To illustrate this point, look what happens to a premium priced retractable after one year.

	Price	Current Yield	Redemption Yield
Today	$31¾	11.2%	6.76%
One year later	$30⅜	11.7%	6.60%

The preferred in this example is callable on 15 February 1987. As it was originally issued with a yield of 14.25% it is an expensive preferred to service. For this reason it could easily be called. Because of the time factor, the preferred must decline in value to maintain its yield to redemption. This is why you should not pay a premium of more than *twenty* per cent for any retractable preferred.

Some retractable preferreds have several retraction dates, while others only have one. Regardless of how many retraction dates there are, after the last (or only one) has passed, the security becomes a *straight preferred*. If you hold any retractables, make a note of all the retraction dates. You don't want to end up with a straight preferred.

When you shop for preferreds it is useful to know the approximate yield spreads between the various types of shares. Regardless of interest rates, straight preferreds yield the most, retractables are in the middle and convertibles yield the least. Here is how they stacked up in the first quarter of 1984:

Straight	Retractable	Convertible
9.5%	8.25%	7.5%

During the past few years some convertible preferreds have come out with a retraction feature. At the same time, some retractable preferreds have enhanced their sales appeal with an equity kicker in the form of warrants to buy common shares of the company. In addition, a number of Canadian retractables have been issued for U.S. dollars, with the option to receive dividends in American or Canadian funds, which provides a currency hedge.

For investors, it has been a rewarding period. Most of my conservative accounts, particularly widows needing income, have done very nicely with retractable and convertible preferreds. But these high yielding securities are not just for widows and orphans. Marvin, one of my largest and most sophisticated clients, has also done well.

Marvin is a high roller who never trades less than five thousand shares. Although he was in good stocks, his portfolio took a battering in the 1981-1982 recession. At the peak of the market, his holdings were worth about ten million dollars. Then came the long slide. As prices fell day after day, Marvin became quite distraught and his health began to suffer. When he finally decided to sell, he took a loss of around three million dollars. The only thing he kept was a hundred thousand shares of Bell. Marvin then left for a protracted holiday in Florida to recover from a bleeding ulcer. While he was down south he decided to change his strategy and become an ultra-conservative investor. During the next year he shrewdly bought large chunks of the best retractable preferred and convertible preferred issues. When the market turned around, Marvin was once again in excellent shape. Having invested in preferreds at the right time, by the end of 1983 he had a profit of more than one million dollars, an assured income, and his old bounce back.

Which just goes to show you, if you choose your preferreds carefully, they can be a damn good investment.

CHAPTER 8

Speculating with Options

MANY INVESTORS THINK options are a crapshooter's delight, or at best a high risk gamble. They certainly can be. Indeed, some experts advise that you avoid them altogether. But options can also increase your income and act as an insurance policy. It all depends on how you use them.

Options have been part of the business scene for centuries. In England the first option transaction on a common stock took place in 1694. But it is only recently that options have been traded on the stock exchanges. In 1973 the Chicago Board Options Exchange became the first exchange in the world to list options. The Chicago Exchange is also the largest option market in the world. The Montreal Exchange began trading options on Canadian stocks in 1975, and the Toronto Stock Exchange commenced option trading a year later. In 1984 the Vancouver Stock Exchange was admitted as a junior partner in the Canadian option market.

An option gives you the right to *buy* or to *sell* something at a *fixed price* for a given period of time. Options are used frequently in the real estate business. If a person is interested in a property, he might offer the owner a fee for the right to buy the property at a set price until a certain date. He might for example pay two thousand dollars for an option on the property until the end of the year. The same principal applies to stock options.

There are two types of stock options, a "call" option and a "put" option. A call option gives you the right to *buy* shares at a fixed price for a fixed period of time, regardless of the market price. A put option is the reverse of a call option. A put option gives you the right to *sell* shares on exactly the same basis.

There are many interesting and profitable ways you can use options, but because they are an entirely different breed of cat from anything we have looked at so far, let me first explain the basics.

A single call or put option represents the right to buy or sell *one hundred shares* of common stock. Thus five calls would represent the right to buy five hundred shares. The fixed price at which the option may be exercised is known as the "strike" price or the "exercise" price. The strike price is described simply by a number, e.g. twenty-five. The term or the length of time the option has to run is identified by the month in which it expires. This may sound vague, but there is a precise date for each security, usually the third Friday in that month. The fee that you pay to buy a stock option or the fee that you receive when you sell one is known as the "premium."

The premium consists of *time* value and *intrinsic* value. When the shares of a company are trading below the strike price, the call option is said to be "out-of-the-money." In this case the premium represents time value, nothing more. When the shares are trading at the strike price, the options are said to be "on-the-money." Here again the premium consists solely of time value. If the shares are trading above the strike price of the calls, the options are described as being "in-the-money." An in-the-money call has both an intrinsic value and a time value. It is easy to determine the amount of the components in the premium. Let's say a call option has a strike price of twenty dollars. The shares are trading at twenty-two and the options are selling at four dollars. Here is the calculation:

Current value of shares	= $22
Strike price of calls	− $20
Intrinsic value of option	$ 2

Cost of option *minus* intrinsic value ($4-$2) = $2 time value
Therefore option consists of $2 intrinsic value + $2 time value

As a general rule, the longer the term of the option, the higher the time value. This makes sense because the longer the term, the more time the underlying shares have to move, and the greater your opportunity for profit. For this reason, as an option approaches its expiry date, the time value begins to dwindle and eventually disappears. So remember, as soon as you buy an option, the clock starts working *against* you.

The longest term of any option is nine months. Options are traded in nine month cycles, and at no time are there more than three expiry dates outstanding. Each company is assigned one of the following cycles:

Cycle 1.	January	April	July	October
Cycle 2.	February	May	August	November
Cycle 3.	March	June	September	December

When an option series expires, a new nine month series begins trading the following day. Thus when the January series expires, trading commences in October options. There is also a formula that if a stock moves up or down by a certain amount, a new strike price will be introduced into the series. For instance in March 1984 Northern Telecom had five different strike prices for its options that expired in April. They were:

April 40
April 45
April 50
April 55
April 60

Your newspaper—if it has a good financial section—will list what options are outstanding, and their prices. Because options are quoted differently than stocks, I have had many clients ask for help in deciphering them. On the opposite page is an example of the standard format, taken from *The Globe and Mail*.

It should be stressed that if you buy an option you are *not* obligated to exercise it. In other words, if you buy five calls you don't have to later pay for five hundred shares. You can sell the calls (hopefully at a profit) or you can simply let them expire. In either case this "closes out" the transaction. By the same token if you sell (which is known as "writing") a call or a put, you can cancel your obligation to deliver or to buy the underlying stock

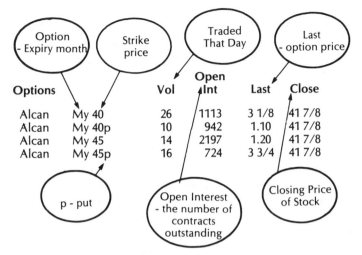

Options		Vol	Open Int	Last	Close
Alcan	My 40	26	1113	3 1/8	41 7/8
Alcan	My 40p	10	942	1.10	41 7/8
Alcan	My 45	14	2197	1.20	41 7/8
Alcan	My 45p	16	724	3 3/4	41 7/8

if you buy back the option *before* it is exercised against you. This can be an expensive solution, but it too will close out the transaction.

Because of the inherent risk in options, there are stringent rules for *both* the broker and the client. To deal in options the broker must take a special course and pass a licencing examination. The client must complete a comprehensive Options Account Application form and sign an Options Trading Agreement. After these forms are signed and accepted by a director of the firm, there is usually a twenty-four hour waiting period before the client can make an option trade. The main purpose of this screening process is to protect the client.

Options do *not* have any margin value, but they may be traded on margin—providing there is a surplus in the margin account to cover the *full amount* of the option transaction. Normally, there is no certificate involved in an option trade. In both Canada and the United States, clearing houses act as custodians for all option trades. (The main clearing house in Canada is Trans Canada Options Inc., while in the U.S. it is the Options Clearing Corporation.) Options also differ from listed stocks in that settlement of all transactions is the following business day. The volatility of the option market is the reason for one day rather than five day settlement.

Only the largest and strongest companies qualify to have options traded on their common shares. The shares of the company must also trade at a value of five dollars or more. This rule recently eliminated one of the most popular options, those of Dome Petroleum. If and when Dome Pete gets its act together, it will be reinstated on the options list. Which brings us to the favourite option game—buying calls on a volatile stock with the hope that the premium will increase in value.

There are several reasons why call options are attractive. Calls are simple to understand: if the underlying stock goes up, so does the price of the calls. When you buy calls on a stock you get tremendous leverage. Take for example a stock trading at twenty dollars. It would cost you twenty thousand dollars to buy one thousand shares. However, if you can buy ten calls at two dollars, you will get the play off the same number of shares for a fraction of the cost. Let us assume that the calls have a strike price of twenty. This is what can happen if the stock goes to twenty-five:

Cost of 1000 shares @ $20 = $20,000 vs. 10 calls @ $2 = $2000
Price of shares rises to $25
1000 shares @ $25 now worth $25,000
10 calls now worth $5 ($20 + $5 = $25) or $5000
Profit on shares = $5000 or <u>25%</u>
Profit on calls = $3000 or <u>150%</u>

In this example I haven't given the premium any time value, but it still shows dramatic leverage. Many options have a significant time value, particularly those on lower priced and volatile stocks.

If you are prepared to accept the risk, I think calls are a good speculation. It makes more sense to gamble on the movement of a senior listed stock—like General Motors—than to take a flier on Old Moose Pasture Mines. At least the game is honest. The advantage of buying calls rather than buying the underlying shares on margin is that you get better leverage, and you will not be required to put up more money if the stock goes down. But remember, you can still lose your *entire* investment, especially if you buy out-of-the-money calls.

Before you buy a call do your homework on the stock. Only *after* you are satisfied that the shares will move higher should you look at the options. Many people make the fundamental error of seizing upon a call option because they think it looks cheap. If you check the stock first, you will usually see why the calls appear cheap. Frequently it is because the underlying shares have declined in price. Sounds obvious, but you would be surprised how many people miss this simple point.

Ideally, a call should have at least six months to run before its expiry date, and the time value in the premium should not be more than ten per cent. From your assessment of the stock the risk/reward ratio should be at least one to two. This means that the calls must have the potential to *double*, because you stand the chance of losing your total outlay.

If you are successful and the price of your calls double, what should you do?

When I was a boy we used to play marbles. If you won the first roll your opponent had to give you his marble. You then pocketed your marble and played with his. The same principle applies to trading options—the first thing to do is to get your marble back, and then play with your winnings. If you buy ten calls that double, here is one way to do it:

Cost of 10 calls @ $3	= $3000
Current price $6	
Sell 5 calls @ $6	− $3000
Retain 5 calls @ cost of	0

This is a conservative strategy. A more aggressive way to get your marble back, but still retain the original number of calls is to "roll up" into a higher strike price. The cost of the new calls may not be exactly half of the original cost, but here is the idea:

Cost of 10 Nov 40 calls @ $3	= $3000
Sell at current price of $6	= $6000
Pocket original investment	− $3000
Balance	= $3000
Buy 10 Feb 45 calls @ $3	= $3000

If you roll up into a higher strike price you will continue to have a play off the same number of calls, but you will be further out-of-the-money. This tactic works well, providing the underlying stock is in a strong uptrend.

Some years ago, when there was a lot of drilling excitement in the Hibernia oil field off Newfoundland, I bought Mobil calls for my own account. In truth I didn't just buy them, I was in and out of them like a crazed ferret. After I got my original investment back, I commenced to roll up with the stock. Each time I went to a higher strike price I took more money out of the market. It seemed so easy. Then I went off for a week with my family to the Cayman Islands. Stupidly, I forgot to put in a stop loss order before I left town. When I got back to Ottawa I found that poor drill results had been released and Mobil shares had plummeted, and so had my calls. I lost about ten thousand dollars. It wasn't a pleasant experience, but it didn't hurt that much because it was all paper profit. Having taken out several times my original investment as I went along, Mobil didn't owe me anything. Had I been less conservative, it would have been a very different story.

I have a client named Ron who is a Member of Parliament. Ron is mesmerized by high risk investments, especially options. When Ron came to me he had lost a lot of money and wanted to win it back in a hurry. I suggested that he be patient and wait for the right opportunity, but this strategy did not appeal to him. We made a few modest sallies into the market and each time turned a small profit. Then we got into Hudson Bay Oil and Gas calls. This was at the time that Dome Pete was rumoured to be about to make a takeover offer. Hudson Bay stock soared and so did the calls. Ron rolled up his strike price but did *not* take out his original investment. Instead, he borrowed money and bought more calls. I pleaded with him to take some profit, but another broker kept telling him to sit tight. Ron listened to the other broker. Eventually the takeover rumour was denied and the bubble burst. Ron couldn't afford to hold his calls and was forced to sell at a loss. (Some months later, Dome Pete actually did make the offer, but by then it was too late.) The moral of this story is that when you have a huge profit in a call option—or any other option—*take it*.

Calls are usually bought as a speculation, but they can also be used as a hedge. For instance, if you are expecting money at some future date (from a mortgage or an inheritance), and intend to buy certain stocks, you can lock in the prices you will pay by buying call options on the shares.

Another strategy, if you already own the underlying stock, is to write (sell) calls to augment your income. If the shares do not trade above the strike price by the expiry date of the calls, the premium you receive is pure profit. Should the calls be exercised, the sale price of your shares will be increased by the amount of the premium you received. For instance, suppose you own five hundred Alcan which is trading at thirty-eight and you write five August forty calls for a premium of two dollars. Your effective sale price in this case is forty dollars plus the two dollar premium, or forty-two dollars per share.

Calls can also be useful if you want to take a tax loss on a stock but still retain the shares. To do this you buy the equivalent number of calls when you sell the shares. Then at a later date you exercise the calls to reinstate your position in the stock. If the underlying shares go up in the meantime, so will the value of your calls.

If you're worried about a particular stock you hold, you can write calls to provide an element of insurance. Using the previous example, with Alcan trading at thirty-eight, the sale of calls at two dollars provides a cushion down to a price of thirty-six dollars per share.

You should only write calls if you are confident that the stock will remain stable or decline in price. Otherwise, for the sake of a few dollars, you will lose your stock and miss out on any decent upward move. It is important to make sure when you write calls that you are satisfied with the total amount—the premium plus the strike price—in the event your calls are exercised.

Dwight and Helen, two of my favourite American clients, make it a practice to write calls on their stocks. This augments their income (as well as mine, because the commissions on options are substantial). In the summer of 1982 Dwight and Helen were largely invested in money market funds. Shortly after the market turned, they asked for stock suggestions and I carefully selected a number of blue chips for them, which they bought. At this point they were well positioned to benefit from the economic recovery. The market surged forward and then had a brief but sharp correction. Some observers, including the panel on "Wall Street Week" prophesied that the market was about to collapse again.

Dwight and Helen are devout followers of "Wall Street Week" and they believed the panel. The following Monday morning Dwight phoned and instructed me to write calls on all their stocks. I didn't think this was very wise, but I learned long ago that it is folly to argue with clients when they have made up their mind to sell. I did as I was told and sold calls on their recently purchased stocks. The average premium they received was around three dollars. In the next six months the market went up several hundred points. Dwight and Helen missed the entire rise, and most of their calls were exercised at strike prices far below the current price of their shares.

This melancholy tale illustrates the negative side of writing calls—if you are wrong, you get some extra income, but the big money is made by the person who *buys* your calls.

You can also earn extra income when you don't own the underlying stock by writing calls. This is known as "uncovered" or more graphically as "naked" writing. It is similar to selling short, but provides more leverage. I would not recommend naked writing because you may be obliged to deliver stock at a much higher price than you sold it for. The risk/reward ratio makes it a very dangerous practice.

If you think a particular stock is going to take a dive, you would be much better to buy puts. This will limit your risk to the amount of the premium you pay, and give you excellent leverage on the downside. If the stock goes up you sell your puts for whatever they will fetch, or let them expire. As explained earlier, a put gives you the right to sell the stock at the strike price for the term of the put. It is the mirror image of a call. Thus as the price of a stock declines, the value of the puts rises. Here is an example of a put transaction compared to a short sale. Let us assume that the stock is trading at $28 and you buy ten puts with a strike price of 27½ for a premium of one dollar. This is what happens if the stock drops to $25:

Short Sale

Proceeds of 1000 shares sold short @ 28	= $28,000
Cost to cover short sale @ 25	− $25,000
Profit on short sale	= $ 3000 or 11%

Put Purchase

Cost of 10 puts with a strike price of 27½ @ $1 = $1000
Price of underlying stock falls to 25
10 puts now worth 2½ (27½ − 25 = 2½) or $2500
Profit on puts = $1500 or 150%

Because of the leverage and the fact that your risk is limited, puts are not only the best but the *safest* way to speculate on the downside. As with buying calls, once you have made a good profit get your original investment back. In the case of puts you roll *down* to a lower strike price as the stock declines. Taking the previous example, you could sell your puts with a strike price of 27½ and, after recovering your investment, buy 10 puts with a 22½ strike price.

Puts are an excellent form of insurance for conservative investors. To protect a gain or prevent a loss you can buy puts with a strike price close to the present level of your shares. If the shares decline, the increase in the value of the puts will largely offset your losses. If later you need to liquidate your holdings, you have two choices: you can exercise your puts or, if it is more advantageous, you can sell *both* your puts and your shares on the market. Should you wish to retain your shares, you simply sell the puts. Investors who would like to take profit in a stock, but can't do so until the following year for tax reasons, can buy long term puts to lock in the profit until they are ready to sell.

Writing puts—which are always "naked"—is a useful way to buy stock at an advantageous price. For instance you might have your eye on the shares of a certain company but feel that at the present level the shares are too expensive. If you write puts, and the puts are exercised against you, the effective cost of the shares will be reduced by the premium you receive for the puts. Let us say that you would like to buy Royal Bank at around twenty-eight but the shares are currently trading at thirty-two. If you wrote April thirty puts for two dollars and the shares were subsequently put to you, your effective cost would be thirty dollars minus the two dollar premium or twenty-eight dollars. Should Royal Bank not decline to your strike price, your puts will not be exercised, and you keep the proceeds from the puts as a consolation prize.

This possibility—that puts will not be exercised—appeals to some hardy investors as a way to increase their income. However, writing puts to increase your income is a high risk strategy, and I would not recommend it to you.

Up to this point we have only dealt with transactions on one side of the market, with one type of option, either a call or a put. There are also a raft of combinations that deal with both sides of the market, involving both calls and puts at the same time. The two main combinations are "straddles" and "spreads." I am not going to discuss "spreads" because I think the main winner in this type of combination is the broker, and I would undoubtedly confuse you (and probably myself) if I tried to explain them. Indeed, I would suggest you *ignore* any complicated strategy.

A "straddle" is a bet on the volatility of a stock. You don't care whether the stock goes up *or* down, you just want a good move in either direction. The ingredients of a straddle consist of a volatile stock, and a call and a put with the *same strike price* and the *same expiry date*. The total cost of the two options, the put and the call, should be as *low* as possible. A straddle will only be profitable after the stock has moved far enough one way or the other to cover the total cost of the put and the call. Here is an example of a straddle. In this case, the underlying stock is trading at forty dollars, and we buy a June forty call for five dollars and a June forty put for three dollars. The total cost of the two options is eight dollars.

> Break even point on upside .... $48   (call worth $8)
> Strike price $40
> Break even point on downside .... $32   (put worth $8)

The only way you can get wiped out on a straddle is if the stock does not move in either direction. Under this set of circumstances, at expiry date both the put and the call would be worthless. (If you chose this type of stock, you shouldn't have done a straddle in the first place.) An ideal situation for a straddle is when a company has a major lawsuit pending and the decision is about to be handed down. Regardless of the outcome, you should get a sharp move in the stock.

Having talked merrily about some of the ways you can use options to make money, I must now tell you that there are less than sixty Canadian companies with listed options. This means that in many promising Canadian situations you won't be able to use options. The option market is much broader in the U.S. and also much more liquid. The Chicago Board Options Exchange lists more than twice as many options as all the exchanges in Canada. For this reason, if you are interested in options, you would be well advised to include U.S. stocks.

It used to be said you can't buy or sell the market, you can only trade in a specific stock. This is no longer true. In the past few years option trading on the stock indices has been introduced. It has proved to be a smashing success. Now, using puts and calls, you can place a bet on the direction of the market. The most popular trading index in the United States is Standard & Poor's (S & P). Actually there are *two* indices, the S & P 500 which is based on five hundred stocks, and the S & P 100 which is based on one hundred stocks.

Both the S & P 500 and the S & P 100 reflect the overall movement of the market by means of a continuously updated index number. For the option player, these numbers are the same as stock prices. At this writing both S & P indices are around 160, and there are options available with strike prices at that figure and on both sides of it.

The underlying security of both S & P indices is a *futures contract* representing the stocks in each index. Futures will be covered in the next chapter so I will not discuss them at this point. However, the value of the S & P 500 contract is five hundred times the number of the index. Therefore if the S & P 500 is trading at 163 the value is 500 × 163 or $81,500US. By the same token, the value of the S & P 100 contract is one hundred times the number of that index. If the S & P 100 is trading at 157 the value would be 100 × 157 or $15,700US.

This information is important because when you buy an S & P

500 call option the cost is *five hundred times* the price of the premium, ie. one call at 3½ would cost $1750. The S & P 100 option—which is by far the most popular—costs the same as any other regular option ie., one hundred times the price of the premium.

For those looking for a fast track, the S & P 100 options trade an incredible volume of contracts each day, and are unquestionably the hottest game in town.

The Toronto Stock Exchange also has options on the TSE 300 Index which represents three hundred listed stocks. I like to buy Canadian whenever possible, but this package is rather dowdy in comparison to the S & P 100 Index.

Both the Toronto and Montreal exchanges have begun trading options on financial futures and commodities. In Toronto you can trade options on Canadian long term bonds, and on silver. The Montreal Exchange has shown the most ingenuity and aggressiveness in developing new options. In addition to options on Canada bonds and silver, the Montreal Exchange trades options on five currencies: the Canadian dollar, the Swiss franc, the German mark, the British pound and the Japanese yen. They also trade in gold options (along with the Vancouver Exchange) and plans are being made to trade options on lumber contracts. If there was a way to write options on the races at Blue Bonnets I'm sure the Montreal Exchange would be in on that, too.

Before leaving the subject of options I would like to stress three points. First, at any given time not more than ten per cent of your portfolio should be invested in options. Second, the option game is a game of opportunity, and you should only play it when an opportunity presents itself. At other times stay on the sidelines. Third, before you decide on a particular option, make a thorough study of the underlying security.

And when you're trading options, don't forget—bulls make money and bears make money—but pigs make none.

CHAPTER 9

Commodity &
Financial Futures

IF YOU LIKE RUSSIAN roulette, you'll love futures. Both provide exciting entertainment. Russian roulette is the game where you load a revolver with a single cartridge, spin the cylinder, and put the muzzle to your temple. As the cylinder contains six chambers and only one is loaded, the odds are five to one that nothing will happen when you pull the trigger. However, the longer you play Russian roulette the more likely you are to blow your brains out. Speculating in futures is much the same in this respect.

Futures are traded on eleven exchanges in the United States and three exchanges in Canada. Trading in futures began on this continent around 1850, and was initially limited to agricultural products. Futures contracts were particularly useful to farmers who faced the problem of not knowing what they would receive for their crops when they were harvested. To ensure a profit, they resorted to selling their crops for delivery at a future date.

A futures contract is a trading unit of a commodity (such as wheat) or a financial instrument (such as a Treasury Bill) for delivery at a specific price on a specific date. The term of the contract ranges from one month to two years. Unlike an option, which gives you the *right* to buy or sell something, a futures contract is a *binding agreement* to take or make delivery of the commodity or financial instrument.

Thus if you short (sell) five cocoa contracts, you have a legal liability to deliver to the buyer fifty metric tons of cocoa. By the same token, if you are long (have bought) two Treasury Bill contracts, you have agreed to buy two million dollars worth of T Bills.

Fortunately, there is a simple way to cancel these obligations. All you have to do is to make an offsetting purchase or sale of the same contract *before* the delivery date. For example, if you had shorted five cocoa contracts, you would buy five contracts. To avoid taking delivery of the Treasury Bills, you would sell two contracts. Approximately ninety-eight per cent of all the contracts written are cancelled by offsetting transactions before the delivery date.

This may sound like an exercise in futility, but it has a genuine commercial application. A futures market, in addition to being a gambling casino, allows *bona fide* producers and users of commodities to reduce the risk of price fluctuations. This type of transaction is known as a "hedge."

The purpose of a hedge is to protect a market commitment by means of an offsetting futures contract. The factors in a hedge are the "cash" or current price and the "forward" or futures price. Normally, the cash price is lower than the forward price due to the time element and storage costs. Because the two prices tend to move parallel, and to converge at delivery date, a loss in one market usually means a profit in the other. What you lose on the swings you will make on the roundabouts. Here is an example of a hedge.

A farmer knows he is going to have wheat to sell in the autumn and wants to ensure that when the crop is harvested he will get an acceptable price. It is May, and even though his crop will not be ready to sell for some months, he would like to get the current "cash" price of $2.10 per bushel. To do this he places a hedge. He sells December futures contracts for the amount of his crop on the commodity exchange. Now he owns or is "long" the wheat (it's growing in his back field) and he is also "short" wheat in the futures market. If the price of wheat is higher by the time he harvests his crop, he will buy back his futures contract and sell his wheat on the cash market. The loss he takes on the repurchase of his futures contract will be offset by the additional profit he makes on the cash market. Here are the figures:

Cash Market	**Futures Market**
12 May	
long wheat @ $2.10 per bu.	Sells wheat @ $2.25 per bu.
1 Nov	
sells wheat @ $2.40 per bu.	Buys wheat @ $2.55 per bu
Profit .30	Loss .30

Even if the price of wheat declines this hedge will still protect him. The profit on the repurchase of his futures contracts will offset the loss on the sale of his wheat in the cash market. Again, here are the figures.

Cash Market	**Futures Market**
12 May	
long wheat @ $2.10 per bu.	sells wheat @ $2.25 per bu.
1 Nov	
sells wheat @ $1.85 per bu.	buys wheat @ $2.00 per bu.
Loss .25	Profit .25

The foregoing was an example of a *selling* hedge. The same principle applies to a *buying* hedge, where the object is to protect the cost of buying a commodity.

A jewellery manufacturer knows in March that he will have to buy five thousand ounces of gold during the summer to manufacture items for the Christmas trade. For this reason he is theoretically short five thousand ounces of gold. He can buy the gold in March, but this would be expensive to carry until manufacturing commences in August. At the same time he can't afford to speculate on the future price of gold, because a rise in the price could wipe out his profit. To protect his margin of profit, which is based on the cash price in March, he buys gold future contacts totalling five thousand ounces for delivery in September. Now he is "short" gold in the cash market and "long" the same amount in the futures market. When August rolls around, he sells the futures contracts and buys the gold on the cash market.

Regardless of the price of gold, his cost will be approximately the same as if he had bought it in March, and his margin of profit will be intact. This is how a buying hedge works:

Cash Market	**Futures Market**
17 Mar	
short gold @ $385 per oz.	buys gold @ $402 per oz.
15 Aug	
buys gold @ $405 per oz.	sells gold @ $422 per oz.
Loss $20	Profit $20

Had the price of gold declined, the effect could have been the same, because the loss in the futures market could have been offset by a profit in the cash market.

Hedging does *not* always work perfectly, as in the foregoing examples, but it does eliminate the risk of drastic price fluctuations. Sometimes a hedge results in a loss and at other times in a profit. It is basically a form of insurance.

You may wonder why it is so easy for hedgers to buy and sell futures. Who is willing to take the risk on the other side of each contract? Usually, it is a speculator. The speculator is not a villain, but a person who performs a vital role by providing liquidity in the commodities markets. He is willing to go long or short, and greases the wheels of commerce by betting against the hedger. Most of the time he is wrong.

In the animal kingdom the speculator could be classed as a "buffer species" or one that is eaten by more powerful animals. The speculator's behaviour is akin to the lemming. This little rodent is preyed upon by hawks and owls as well as a host of valuable fur bearers. Periodically, lemmings are seized by an urge to rush headlong to their destruction. When this happens, many of them are marooned on the ice or drown in the sea. It is not clear why lemmings engage in this unfortunate practice, but we do know what motivates the speculator. The chance of a fat profit.

Very little money is needed to buy or sell a futures contract. Often the margin requirement is less than five per cent of the value of the contract. Because the margin is in fact a performance bond or "earnest money," no interest is charged on the balance. This gives stupendous leverage. Commissions are also seductively attractive in that they are much lower than for stocks, and only one commission is charged instead of two. The single commission is known as a "round turn" and is levied when you liquidate your position.

Speculators make money when they correctly judge the price movement of a particular commodity. Usually, they only play one side of the market. If they think the price is going to rise they buy the commodity; if they think it is going to fall, they short it.

Let us suppose you are a speculator and you think the price of soybeans will rise. In April you go long (buy) two November contracts at $7.30. As each contract represents five thousand bushels, you now own ten thousand bushels of soybeans. The margin on this purchase is $2500 per contract or $5000. The price of soybeans goes up, and in October you sell your contracts for $8.06 per bushel. Here are the figures on the transaction:

10 April	bought 2 November	
	soybeans @	$7.30
	(Margin $5000)	
7 September	sold 2 November	
	soybeans @	$8.06
	Profit per bushel	.76
	10,000 bushels × 76 cents	= $7600
	Commission	−$ 182
	Net profit	$7418 or 148%

Speculating on the short side of the market can also be lucrative. For instance, you might think the price of pork is too high and is bound to fall. In June you short (sell) three February pork belly contracts at sixty-three cents per pound. One pork belly contract represents 38,000 pounds, thus you are short 114,000 pounds of bacon. The margin on this sale is $1500 per contract or $4500. By December, the price of February bellies has declined significantly. At that time you cover your short position by buying three February contracts at fifty-five cents per pound. This is your profit on the transaction:

6 June	sold 3 February pork	
	bellies @	.63
	(Margin $4500)	
21 December	bought 3 February pork	
	bellies @	.55
	Profit per pound	.08
	114,000 pounds × 8 cents =	$9120
	Commission	–$ 270
	Net profit	$8850 or 196%

The foregoing examples show the bright side of speculating in futures contracts. I must warn you that there is also a dark side to the game. Leverage is a two-edged sword which can produce staggering *losses* as well as glorious profits. If you are wrong you can not only lose the shirt off your back, but all the other shirts you own. So before you reach for the phone to cash in on this bonanza it might be prudent to examine the futures market in greater detail.

If you are going to get into the futures market you should choose a firm that *specializes* in commodity trading. In Canada, relatively few investment dealers engage in this type of business. Among those who do are Richardson Greenshields, Bache, and, of course, "The Thundering Herd" (Merrill Lynch). Burns Fry, the firm that I am with, tends to concentrate on financial instruments and is a major player on the Toronto Futures Exchange.

The individual you select to manage your account should devote most of his time to the futures market. (To deal in futures a broker must have a special licence which is only granted to those who pass a rigorous examination.) If your regular broker is not licenced, or only trades commodities as a sideline—as I do—open an account with someone else.

When opening an account you will be required to complete and sign a number of forms. One of the crucial questions you will be asked concerns the amount of your liquid assets. Liquid assets are cash and negotiable securities—your house, even if it is fully paid for, is *not* a liquid asset. Do not fudge the answer because the broker will check with your bank to confirm that your estimate of liquid assets is correct. (In Ottawa recently, a prominent Member of Parliament was turned down by a broker as a result of a phone call to his bank.) The stress on liquid assets should tell you something: the broker wants to be sure that you can come up with more money after you have lost all or part of your margin deposit. Most brokers will not open a futures account unless you have *at least* fifty thousand dollars in liquid assets.

The minimum margin requirement for each commodity is set by the exchange on which it is traded. However, many brokers have house rules that call for higher margin. Also, if a commodity becomes very volatile, the margin can be raised without prior notice.

Actually there are *two* margin levels to consider. The first is "initial margin" which is the opening amount, and the second is "maintenance margin" which is a lower figure. Once the maintenance level has been violated, your account must be topped up to the initial margin. For example, the initial margin for a contract of rapeseed (which is a popular trader on the Winnipeg Commodity Exchange) is three hundred dollars, and the maintenance margin is two hundred dollars. This gives you a cushion of one hundred dollars, but if the price of rapeseed moves against you and the cushion is punctured, you will receive a margin call. When this happens you must immediately put up more money, or you will be sold out.

Because the margin on commodities is a performance bond rather than a partial payment, you can pledge Treasury Bills instead of cash. This permits you to earn a return on your deposit. If you are trading on U.S. exchanges, all transactions, including your margin, must be in American funds.

Let us assume that you have cleared the hurdles and have opened a commodities account. Now you are looking around for something to trade. Here is a partial list of the commodities and financial instruments you can choose from:

Aluminum   Barley   Bonds   Broilers   Cattle   Cocoa
Coffee   Copper   Corn   Cotton   Crude Oil   Currencies

Eggs   Eurodollars   Flaxseed   Gold   Heating Oil   Hogs
Lumber   Mortgage Rates   Oats   Orange Juice
Palladium   Platinum   Plywood   Pork Bellies   Potatoes
Propane   Rapeseed   Rye   Silver   Soybean Meal
Soybean Oil   Soybeans   Stock Indices   Sugar
Treasury Bills   Wheat

As you can see, there is something for every taste. However, not all of these commodities are active traders, and if you are a speculator you should restrict your choice to a commodity or financial instrument that has good volume and is highly liquid—so you can get in and *out* easily. It is also wise to pick a commodity that trades on one of the busier exchanges.

In Canada, the Winnipeg Commodities Exchange dominates the market for agricultural products. Winnipeg was also the first commodity exchange in the world to trade gold. The recently opened Toronto Futures Exchange is Canada's main market for financial instruments. Montreal plans to trade financial futures, but at this writing it is primarily concerned with *options* on currencies and precious metals.

In the United States—which is the best place for speculators to play—the Chicago Board of Trade is the largest commodity exchange. It is mainly a market for agricultural products but it also trades U.S. Treasury bonds. The Chicago Mercantile Exchange and its subsidiary, the International Monetary Market, are also active trading arenas for commodities and financial instruments. The Comex (Commodity Exchange Inc.) of New York is the busiest metals market in the world.

When you give a commodity order to your broker it will be processed with the same speed as a stock order. Instead of going to a stock exchange, it will be wired to the appropriate commodity exchange. The order will be executed in a trading "pit" by open outcry, and the confirmation will be wired back to your broker, who in turn will relay the news to you.

It should be noted that the contract size can vary with the exchange. Therefore, *before* you enter your order make sure of the contract size. Gold for instance, trades on the Winnipeg Exchange in 20 ounce contracts, while the Chicago Board of

Trade has two gold contracts: one for 32.15 ounces (one kilo) and the other for 100 ounces.

Having established a speculative position—either long or short—you can't just forget it. If you do, you could get an unpleasant surprise. I should mention that the nightmare of having one hundred tons of soybean meal dumped on your front lawn will not happen. If you let a long position go to the delivery date you will receive a warehouse notice stating that the commodity is being held for you. For a price, someone will buy the warehouse receipt and assume custody of the contract. By the same token, if you are short a commodity at delivery date, you can usually cover your obligation to deliver—again, at a price.

One spectacular exception occurred in 1980 when Nelson Bunker Hunt and his family nearly "cornered" the market for silver. After buying for months, Hunt and his colleagues demanded physical delivery of silver that had been shorted to them. This short "squeeze" caused the price of silver to sky-rocket, and forced the shorts to the wall. Hunt might have succeeded in cornering the market if the authorities had not changed the delivery rules and let the shorts off the hook. When this happened, the price of silver collapsed.

Aside from phoning your broker periodically, you can keep track of your investment by checking the financial section of the newspaper. Only the larger newspapers cover commodities, and if your paper doesn't provide this information I would recommend that you subscribe to one that does. On page 114 is an example of the way commodities are quoted in the paper.

If you want to value the move in a commodity, multiply the size of the contract by the change in its price. Taking Soybean Meal as an example, the contract size is one hundred tons, therefore a change of one dollar per ton is equal to one hundred dollars per contract. In the following table, a May contract would have declined by $130, a July contract by $120 and an August contract by $60.

To prevent wild daily price fluctuations the exchanges establish trading limits for each commodity. Once the commodity has reached its limit—either on the upside or the downside—no

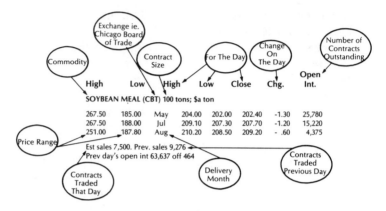

SOYBEAN MEAL (CBT) 100 tons; $a ton

High	Low		High	Low	Close	Chg.	Open Int.
267.50	185.00	May	204.00	202.00	202.40	-1.30	25,780
267.50	188.00	Jul	209.10	207.30	207.70	-1.20	15,220
251.00	187.80	Aug	210.20	208.50	209.20	- .60	4,375

Est sales 7,500. Prev. sales 9,276
Prev day's open int 63,637 off 464

transactions are permitted above or below the limit. If Orange Juice futures close at $1.70 per pound and the limit is five cents (with a maximum range of ten cents), no trades can take place the following day above $1.75 or below $1.65. This may sound like a comfort, but the limit rule can cause acute anxiety.

Suppose you are short orange juice futures, and a sudden frost blankets Florida, killing much of the crop. Because this unforseen development will affect the supply in the coming months—driving up the price—you decide to "cover" your short position. To do this, you enter an order to buy offsetting contracts. When the market opens, the bid for orange juice futures immediately moves up to the limit, but no one is willing to sell at that price. You are "locked in" and there is nothing you can do about it. The next day the same thing happens, the bid moves up to the limit but still no one is willing to sell. By this time you are sweating blood. Finally, on the third day, the exchange expands the limit by fifty per cent, and you manage to cover your short position at a heavy loss.

You can get into the same bind when you are long a commodity, and it makes "locked" limit moves on the downside for several days in succession. However, if you own a stock and it takes the gas, you can always get out at a lower price. Trading commodities is *not like trading stocks.* Keep this in mind.

This brings us to the factors that influence the price of commodities. These factors can be divided into three basic categories: Economic, Political and Acts of God. I don't propose to dwell on these factors, but I will give an example of each one.

The demand for copper, one of the most volatile commodities, is directly related to the state of the economy. Roughly half of the copper produced is used by the electrical industry, the rest by other industrial consumers such as the construction and automobile industries. As a result, both the demand for copper and its price rise when the economy is buoyant, and fall during periods of recession.

Wheat is a volatile commodity, which is influenced by international politics. The United States and Canada are the world's largest exporters of wheat. Among the major importers are Russia, China, and the Communist bloc countries. When North America exports a substantial amount of wheat, the domestic supply is reduced and prices rise. When Russia and the U.S. are at loggerheads, large export contracts may be cancelled or delayed, which has the reverse effect.

Acts of God encompass weather phenomena and other natural disasters. Frost in the Citrus Belt, drought on the Prairies, and floods in the Cotton Bowl are all fairly common. One of the most bizarre was the disappearance of the anchovy school off Peru a few years ago which was caused by a shift in the Humboldt Current. This resulted in a dramatic price increase for soybean meal futures. Soybean meal is exported as a high protein supplement for poultry and livestock. Peru competes for this market by exporting fish meal made from anchovies. When the anchovies failed to show up off Peru, the demand for soybean meal soared.

Physical commodities—such as grains, livestock, and other produce—are subject to economic, political, and natural influences. Financial instruments—such as bonds, currencies, and stock indices—are somewhat more predictable in that Acts of God are not a major factor. The main considerations with financial futures are the economic and political factors. This makes their price movements difficult to judge, but not impossible.

I would suggest that if you must speculate in commodities, you start with financial futures. Financial futures permit you to bet on the direction of the American and Canadian stock markets, the trend of interest rates, and movements in the world's major currencies. Hedging and "spreading" techniques (which are also applicable to physical commodities) can reduce but not eliminate your potential for loss. If you are already in the stock or bond market, experience will have taught you something about the financial situation.

On the other hand, if you start by trading physical commodities, you may be severely handicapped by a lack of knowledge. For instance, unless you are a pig farmer, or run an abattoir, it is unlikely you will have an informed opinion on pork bellies.

Whatever you choose to trade—whether it be a financial instrument or a physical commodity—you would be well advised to follow some guidelines. Here are a few suggestions which you might consider:

—do your homework on a commodity *before* entering an order.

—always go *with* the trend, don't try to outguess the market.

—limit your involvement in any single investment to a maximum of 10% of your speculative capital.

—spread your risk over two or three commodities, and watch them closely.

—select contracts in the more distant maturities. They are usually less volatile and give you more time.

—when you open a trade have a specific profit in mind. If your target is reached, close out the transaction.

—protect your position with a stop loss order. If you are long and the price increases, move the stop price up. If you are short and the price declines, move the stop down.

—do not pyramid your winnings by buying or selling additional contracts, unless you literally want to go for broke.

—when you get a margin call, close out the position. You are wrong, and if you put up more money the odds are that you will lose it.

—do not average down. This is a sucker's game.

—when you are wrong do *not* reverse your position. You can easily get "whip-sawed" (lose in both directions).

—take your losses quickly, but *let your profits run.* One big win can erase a lot of little losses.

—don't feel compelled to be in the market all the time. Often, the smartest thing is to watch from the sidelines.

These suggestions will not make you rich beyond the dreams of avarice, but they may keep you out of serious trouble. If you're a speculator, and you can stay out of trouble you are doing well. It is generally conceded that between eighty and ninety per cent of speculators eventually lose *all* their money. Also, I have been told by brokers who deal exclusively in commodities that they have to replace their clientele three to four times a year. The reason for this turnover is financial "burn-out." That term needs no explanation.

Consider my friend Charles for instance. Charles is a highly intelligent man with an impressive list of achievements. At university he not only graduated at the top of his class in *two* professions, but he was also a star athlete. He had a short but successful professional career, and then became a partner in a high tech company. He subsequently sold his shares in the company and retired with more than a million dollars.

With time and money on his hands, Charles turned to the stock market. He did well, but he found it rather boring. Eventually, he turned to the commodities market. This he found fascinating. After his initial losses, he decided that the only way to play commodities was by mathematical logic. To this end he purchased a computer, and assembled a data base that covered the last seventy years. He began this project in 1978.

I visited Charles at his house a few weeks ago. The walls of his study were covered with charts, the bookshelves were stuffed with hundreds of volumes of market reports, and he now had two computers. (Because he had run out of space, some of his computer hardware and tapes were stored in an adjacent bathroom.) Charles does not trade with a local broker, but places his business directly through a discount house in Chicago. He told me that sometimes his orders are filled within thirty seconds. Charles proudly showed me his latest acquisition, a computer link with the floor of the Comex that prints a graph showing the minute to minute moves on gold, silver, and copper. At that time Charles was playing silver futures, as he had been for some months.

I was awed by his computers and his incredible store of information. Here was a man who obviously had the commodities market by the tail. Over drinks I asked him how he had done in the past six years. Charles thought for a moment and then replied: "I've had a lot of fun, but of course, I've lost money."

His answer confirmed a long held suspicion of mine. Unless you are a trader in the "pit" or an insider, your chance of making money in commodities is almost nil.

The next time you get the urge to go long wheat or pork bellies, do *not* phone your broker. Instead, trot down to your neighbourhood supermarket and buy a loaf of bread or a pound of bacon. This is the best commodity tip I can give you.

CHAPTER 10

Mutual Funds

IF YOU DON'T KNOW how to bake a cake, or don't have the ingredients, you can buy a cake mix. This eliminates work on your part and is guaranteed to produce a cake. It may not be as good as the ones Mother used to bake, but it will be quite acceptable. The same applies to mutual funds. If you don't know anything about investing, or don't have the money to buy a portfolio of stocks, you can buy a mutual fund. Some mutual funds are bland but others are surprisingly good. It depends upon which one you choose.

A mutual fund is company or a trust whose assets consist of securities. These securities are managed for the benefit of the shareholders. Thus a shareholder of a mutual fund owns a small piece of a large investment portfolio.

Therein lies the appeal of a mutual fund. By investing as little as a few hundred dollars, you can get both diversification and professional management. After you plunk down your money, you can forget about it because your investment is looked after by someone else.

There are two types of mutual funds: "Open-End" and "Closed-End." The most common, and the one that we will concentrate on in this chapter, is the Open-End fund.

An Open-End fund does not have a fixed capitalization, but continuously offers and redeems its shares. Normally, the shares are redeemed at their actual value, which is known as the "Net

Asset Value," and sold at a premium above the Net Asset Value. Because Open-End funds make their own market and deal directly with the public, their shares are not listed on the stock exchanges.

Closed-End funds (which are also called Investment Trusts) are like regular corporations in that they have a fixed number of shares which are listed on the exchange or traded over-the-counter. They may also have bonds, preferred shares, and warrants outstanding. Unlike the shares of Open-End funds, the shares of Closed-End funds can trade at a premium or a discount to their Net Asset Value. Usually they trade at a discount. The reason for the discount is that investors know the fund is unlikely to liquidate all its assets and distribute the proceeds to its shareholders.

As a matter of interest, there are two types of Closed-End funds. Investment companies—like Canadian General Investments or United Corporations—are one type. Investment companies simply supervise a portfolio of securities. The other type, holding companies—such as British Columbia Resources Investment Corporation or Brascan—own controlling blocks of companies and take an active part in their management.

But let's get back to Open-End mutual funds. In Canada there are approximately two hundred funds in this category. As one might expect, their investment objectives range from safety and income to outright speculation. Both the *Financial Times* and *The Financial Post* cover mutual funds, but the most comprehensive information is found in the monthly survey of funds by the *Financial Times*. If you study this survey you can get an excellent handle on what's available, and how the funds stack up against each other.

For purposes of comparison the *Financial Times* breaks the funds into four divisions:

Equity Funds   Guaranteed Income Funds
Fixed Income Funds   Gold Specialty Funds

The funds in each division are segregated as to whether they are eligible or not eligible for tax shelter. Eligibility depends upon the percentage of the fund's foreign investments. If a fund qualifies for tax shelter, it may be purchased for a Registered Retirement Savings Plan without restriction. *This is important* because under current legislation an RRSP can't hold more than ten per cent of its assets in foreign securities or a mutual fund that is largely invested in foreign securities.

Equity funds are those that consist mainly of equities or common shares. As a result, they are the most volatile. To help readers assess the risk, the *Financial Times* gives its list of equity funds a "variability" rating. Variability refers to the degree of their price fluctuation. High Variability funds are the big swingers who outperform the market on the upside, but fare worse than the averages on the downside. Funds in the Intermediate category are more sedate and tend to move parallel with the general market. Those in the Low Variability group show the smallest swings and give the most consistent—but not the best—rates of return.

The *Financial Times* survey shows each fund's rate of return for the past year, as well as the past three years, five years, and ten years. Rate of return is measured by taking the gain on the Net Asset Value of the shares, with dividends reinvested, from the start of the period to the present. If we take AGF Special Fund Limited as an example, here are the figures at 31 January 1984. (AGF Special Fund is an equity fund in the High Variability group, without tax eligibility.)

Assets in $ millions	% Invested in foreign securities	Sales Fee range	Annual Compound Rate of return			
			1 yr.	3 yr.	5 yr.	10 yr.
53.3	84	2.00 – 9.00	18.8	17.6	27.7	23.0

It should be stressed that the quality of management varies with each fund, and management personnel change from time to time. In addition, a fund's past results *do not* mean that its performance will be the same in the future. Also, when comparing funds pay particular attention to the five and ten year figures. These show whether a fund has performed *consistently* over the long haul. Don't be carried away by a stunning performance over the past year—it may be a fluke or a flash in the pan. What you are looking for is a fund that has an above average rate of return for both the long and the short term. The example I have used, AGF Special Fund, meets this requirement and is one of the top performers in its category.

Once you have isolated an equity fund which you think has a good record, you should compare its performance with another yardstick, the Toronto Stock Exchange 300 Index. (If you don't do this additional step you may find you have merely chosen the best of a bad lot.) The TSE 300 Index is comprised of three hundred stocks listed on the Toronto Stock Exchange. This group includes a grab bag of good, bad, and indifferent companies which together reflect the average price level of the exchange. When you make this test you will be surprised to see how many equity funds—managed by highly paid experts—have not been able to match the performance of the TSE 300 Index.

Canadian Investment Fund (which is in the Intermediate Variability group, with tax shelter eligibility) is a case in point. CIF has more than one hundred million in assets and is Canada's oldest mutual fund. It also has the most distinguished board of directors of any fund in the country. This makes pleasant reading in the prospectus, but has not done much for the Net Asset Value of the fund's shares. Over the long term CIF has underperformed the TSE 300 Index.

Fixed Income funds invest in debt securities such as bonds, debentures, mortgages, Treasury Bills, certificates of deposit, and the like. They offer little in the way of capital gain, but can produce an acceptable overall return—most of which is taxable. You can also buy Guaranteed Income mutual funds, which have a guaranteed minimum rate of return. I can't see any reason to buy a Guaranteed Income fund when a government bond will give you greater safety, a similar return, and complete liquidity.

The most interesting development in the income group is the recent introduction of Money Market funds. This type of fund, which is very popular in the United States, invests in Treasury Bills and other short term securities. Normally there is no charge to buy a Money Market fund, and even with the management fee, the rate of return is often as good or better than you could get elsewhere.

Before you purchase a fund, do your homework. Read the latest annual or quarterly report to learn what type of securities are in the fund's portfolio. Study the prospectus carefully. This is *very* important. The prospectus will give you all sorts of information, including the objectives of the fund and the conditions attached to the purchase and redemption of its shares. The latter should be scrutinized with a beady eye, because the terms differ from fund to fund.

Net Asset Value relates to both the purchase price and the redemption price of the fund's shares. It is calculated by taking the fund's assets (cash and securities) and deducting the total liabilities. The number of the fund's shares is then divided into the balance to get the Net Asset Value per share. Here is an example:

Value of securities	$10,000,000
Plus cash	$ 1,000,000
Total	$11,000,000
Less total liabilities —	$ 3,000,000
Net assets	$ 8,000,000
Number of outstanding shares 1,200,000	
Divide 1,200,000 shares into $8,000,000	
Net Asset Value per share	= $6.66

Most mutual funds offer their shares at a premium to the Net Asset Value. This premium usually ranges from nine per cent to two per cent, and is based on a sliding scale. The larger the purchase, the lower the premium. Here is a typical sales schedule:

Amount of Purchase	Premium Charged
Up to $9,999	9%
$10,000 to $24,999	8%
$25,000 to $49,999	6.5%
$50,000 to $99,999	5%
$100,000 to $199,999	4%
$200,000 to $299,999	3%
$300,000 to $499,999	2%
Over $500,000	Negotiable

As you can see the commission charges are stiff. This makes

the purchase of mutual fund shares a *long term* investment. The reason is that you will need time to recoup the sales charge. Put another way, if you pay an eight per cent premium it's like entering a race with a handicap. If it's a hundred yard dash, you are eight yards behind the starting line when the gun goes off. But if you are eight yards behind the starting line on the mile run, you should be able to erase the handicap over the distance.

Mutual funds are sold directly by the funds (some of whom have their own sales personnel), brokers, trust companies, banks, and money management companies. Unlike stocks, there is no need or advantage to buying in board lots. The funds are quite happy to sell you fractional shares.

Normally a purchase is done on the basis of a lump sum, ie., $5000 rather than the number of shares. In the case of a lump sum purchase, the sales charge is levied on the gross amount, which actually *increases* the effective rate of commission. Let us say you are going to buy five thousand dollars worth of a fund whose Net Asset Value is ten dollars per share, and eight per cent is the premium charged for that amount. You would think that this would be eighty cents per share and your cost would therefore be $10.80. But it doesn't work out that way. Here are the figures:

Cost of purchase	= $5000
Less 8%	− $ 400
Balance remaining to buy shares	$4600
@ $10 per share buys 460 shares	
460 divided into $5000 = $10.87 per share	
Effective premium is	8.7%

Except by negotiation—which is only feasible if you are buying large amounts—it is difficult to beat the system. Had you stipulated that you wanted to buy 460 shares of the fund, rather than five thousand dollars worth, it would still cost you five thousand dollars. There is a formula (which I am not going to bore you with) that justifies a price of $10.87 per share.

Having made a lump sum purchase, the worst is behind you. In most cases when you sell your shares the fund will redeem them from you at the Net Asset Value with no further charges.

You can also buy mutual funds on a contractual basis by signing up to pay so much per month for a period of years. The commissions on contractual sales fall into three graphically descriptive categories: Front-End Load, Level Load, and Rear-end Load. Front-End Load means that a large part of your first year's installments will go to paying commission rather than to buying shares in the fund. Level Load means that the commission—which may be as high as twelve per cent—will be distributed evenly over the term of the contract. Rear-End Load (which is rare) means that you will pay the commission when the shares are redeemed. You would be well advised to avoid contractual plans like the plague.

Some mutual funds offer their shares to the public with *no sales charge.* You might wonder how this is possible, and if they don't charge a commission how they can make money. First, let me assure you that they do make money. The cost of selling "no load" mutual funds is lower because no sales force is maintained and advertising is kept to a minimum. Many are sold over the counter by banks and trust companies. So it's less expensive to sell them. The management company of a "no load" fund, whether it be a corporation or a financial institution, makes its profit by charging shareholders a relatively high annual fee for managing the assets. Also, when you sell your shares in a "no load" fund you will usually find that there is a fee charged for redemption. As I said earlier, it is difficult to beat the system. Nevertheless, if you are trying to choose between two funds *with a similar performance record,* and one is a "no load" fund, it will probably be the best buy.

Why should you buy a mutual fund? There are a number of sound reasons. The most obvious is to get professional management and diversification with a small amount of money. Another is to acquire a "package" of securities in a particular industry or commodity. For instance there are mutual funds that specialize in high tech stocks, oil and gas securities, commodities, options and precious metals. (Gold funds will be covered in the next chapter.) Even for the sophisticated investor, mutual funds are a good way to participate in foreign markets, particularly the United States and Japan. Buying a fund which holds foreign securities gives you a double play, because you are speculating on the *currency* as well as the stocks in the portfolio. Being long term investments, mutual funds are well suited to Registered Retirement Savings Plans.

The entire investment community—which includes banks, trust companies, money management firms, and insurance companies as well as brokers—is well aware that mutual funds and Registered Retirement Savings Plans go together like ham and eggs. Indeed, each year a campaign is mounted to attract RRSP contributions into mutual funds. It is invariably successful, and mutual fund sales soar during this period.

The campaign starts on the first of January. That morning thousands of bleary-eyed Canadians realize that the year is over and they must do something about their Registered Retirement Savings Plan. If they don't make a contribution, they will pay more tax. Figuratively clutching $3500 to $5500 in their hands they rush out to find a suitable investment.

The investment community is ready and waiting for them. At the bank a smiling teller asks if they would like to buy a mutual fund or a term deposit. The trust company on the corner has taken down its sign in the window offering "A Merry Guaranteed Investment Certificate" as the ideal Christmas gift for a loved one and replaced it with an equally large sign offering mutual funds and *free* RRSP advice. On the radio, the money management companies exhort listeners to come and see them without obligation. The insurance companies get into the act with clever (insured) investments specially designed for Registered Retirement Savings Plans.

Even brokers, including some of those who normally cater to the carriage trade and wouldn't look at an account of $3500 to $5500, suddenly become enthusiastic about mutual funds. (The fact that nine per cent of $5500 is $495—a respectable commission—may be a contributing factor.) Brokers bombard their clients with literature and take out huge ads in the paper. It is the only time in the year that they spend this money extolling the virtues of a mutual fund. As one wag said to me "Little fish taste sweet."

The pace becomes increasingly hectic as the deadline of the first of March approaches, both for the taxpayer and the investment community. It reminds me of a drama in nature known as a bluefish "blitz." The bluefish is a powerful ocean fish with a voracious appetite. Even after they have eaten their fill they will continue to chomp through a school of baitfish. Bluefish are particularly fond of small herring, and when they encounter a shoal in shallow water all hell breaks loose. I have seen this happen many times. If you are standing on the beach you will suddenly see little silver fish darting out of the water. Seconds later bluefish erupt in the middle of the school like hand grenades. The commotion on the surface attracts gulls who seem to appear from nowhere. The noisy gulls add to the frenzy by wheeling and diving on the hapless herring. It is a scene of sound and fury. The carnage ends as suddenly as it began, when the herring move out to deeper water.

The same thing happens on the first of March with the mutual fund campaign. The financial community's feeding spree ends. For the next ten months mutual funds resume their place —as just another investment.

CHAPTER 11

Gold

GOLD. IF YOU'RE BEING ignored at a cocktail party, just drop that word. It's sure to gain attention. Gold has a mystical quality that excites and fascinates people. Since the days of the Pharaohs gold has symbolized wealth, and in many parts of the world it represents the ultimate refuge against economic disaster.

Gold is very rare. Although it has been mined for five thousand years, all the gold in existence would fit into four Olympic sized swimming pools. For centuries gold has been used to make jewellery. It is ideal for this purpose because it has a natural lustre, it is non-allergenic, it resists corrosion, and it is highly malleable. Indeed, one ounce of the yellow metal can be drawn into a wire fifty miles long or beaten into a sheet covering one hundred square feet.

Gold is also an excellent conductor of heat and electricity. These properties, combined with its softness and reflective quality, have important applications in the space age. Today gold is used extensively in the computer and electronic industries.

While it is coveted for industrial and decorative purposes, gold's main role is that of a medium of exchange. Unlike paper money, gold needs no one's signature to make it valuable. Many countries back their currencies with vast holdings of gold. The largest gold reserve is held by the United States.

In 1934 the United States pegged the price of gold at $35.00

per ounce. This continued until 1968 when mounting economic pressures forced the seven nation Gold Pool to establish a two tier market. Under the two tier system gold was traded between governments at $35 per ounce but between everyone else at whatever the market would bear. In 1970 the U.S. increased the official price of gold to $38 (which amounted to a devaluation of the American dollar) and again in 1973 raised the price of gold to $42.22 per ounce. On 1 January 1974 American citizens were allowed for the first time in forty years to own gold. It was at this point that the free market began to flourish and the price of gold started its dramatic rise.

Those who fervently believe in gold are know as "gold bugs." My first encounter with a gold bug was in 1968. At that time gold was trading around $40 an ounce, and few people took any notice of the yellow metal. One of the few who did was Cecil, a nervous little man with a bald head and bright blue eyes. Cecil was certain that gold was going to triple or quadruple in value, and to convince me he would quote from the writings of Franz Pick and other zealots. Often he would get so excited that he could hardly get the words out fast enough. I listened to Cecil politely, because I like him and he was a good client. But privately I suspected he was not playing with a full deck, and I knew he was wrong.

As it turned out, Cecil was right. Within the next five years the price of gold tripled and then quadrupled. In 1980 gold in New York touched $825 an ounce, and in London it hit $850 an ounce. It has since settled back, but in the spring of 1984 gold is still ten times higher than it was in 1968.

What cause this astounding increase? Unpegging gold allowed the price to catch up with other commodities, but the explosive move was brought about by entirely different factors. Because fear is the principal motive for owning gold, political turmoil—such as the Russian invasion of Afghanistan—frightened people into buying gold. Fear of currency devaluations in a number of countries (which subsequently happened) also drove people into gold to protect their assets. But the main reason, and what really fueled the price rise, was skyrocketing inflation. This was aggravated by the soaring cost of oil. Having been paid in paper currencies for their oil, Mid-East countries then turned around and bought gold. Speculators saw the price of gold take off, and jumped aboard for the ride. The result was a runaway gold market.

The market collapsed because of the excesses that were built into it. Although there were further political incidents, such as the war in the Falklands, and more devaluations, the tide of inflation began to recede. Because the rate of inflation was declining, gold did not respond in a positive way to these events. This highlights the behaviour of gold and the main reason for owning it—*as a hedge against inflation*.

Gold is a hedge against inflation because over the centuries it has retained its purchasing power. Historians note that the same amount of gold will buy the same amount of wheat that it did two hundred years ago. This may not seem impressive, but consider paper money. Pick any currency you want—the Canadian dollar for example. Now look back ten years, and remember how much it cost you to buy a loaf of bread. This will show you how, in the space of just ten years, inflation has eroded the value of the dollar.

Inflation will continued to ravage the dollar so long as the federal government spends more than it receives in taxes. Deficits produce debt that the government finances by simply creating more money. When money is pumped into the system in this way it dilutes the existing currency. Eventually *all the currency in circulation* loses some of its purchasing power or real value. Because of reckless spending, inflation is now deeply embedded in the Canadian economy. The only variable is its annual rate of growth. It should also be mentioned that many countries with high rates of inflation have been forced to devalue their currencies. This happens without warning, and causes hardship to everyone.

Radical gold bugs are certain that inflation will inevitably lead to the collapse of the economy. This in turn will bring about the fall of the government. With people out of work and starving, law and order will break down and the result will be chaos. To survive this situation radical gold bugs advise you to convert all your paper money into gold. Having done this, you should build a fortress in your basement and provision it for a long siege. In addition to the necessities of life (and your gold), the bunker should contain arms and ammunition to keep insurgents at bay. To buy provisions during the crisis you should also have a few bags of "junk" silver coins. (Junk coins are old coins with a genuine silver content). When order is restored you convert your gold into hard currency and go on your merry way.

Although I do not wish to nitpick, there are a few tiny flaws in this recipe for survival. Let us suppose you are safely ensconced in your bunker. Your food is running low and you are feeling somewhat peckish, so you decide to go out and buy a steak. You pluck a 1946 quarter out of your bag of junk silver, strap your pistol around your waist, and emerge from your den. Blinking in the sunlight like a mole, you find yourself surrounded by a desperate mob looting and pillaging among the ruins of your neighbourhood.

Now let us stop here for a moment.

Do you think that these bad people, knowing that you have *real* money in your hand, will clear a path so that you can sashay to the supermarket? Will there be a supermarket to go to? If the answer is no to either of these questions, what will you do with your 1946 quarter? You can't eat it.

As you may have guessed, I am not a radical or even a garden variety gold bug. However, I do think that it is prudent to have some of your assets invested in gold. The amount you invest is up to you. Personally, I would not commit more than twenty-five per cent of my assets to gold. Remember that equities, especially resource stocks, are also an inflation hedge. So is your house.

Silver is also a good inflation hedge. Silver is much more plentiful than gold, and hence less valuable. There is no fixed price spread between the two precious metals, but gold and silver are inclined to move in unison. Like gold, silver is an excellent conductor of heat and electricity—in fact, it is the most efficient conductor of any metal. For this reason silver is widely used by the electrical and photographic industries, as well as for jewellery, coins, and utensils. At present, the consumption of silver exceeds the annual world production of the metal.

A fundamental difference between gold and silver is that a large amount of the silver used by industry is lost forever, whereas gold is carefully recycled. Millions of ounces of silver are "lost" or consumed in camera film. Gold, on the other hand, is melted down and survives from generation to generation. An example of gold recycling occurred in Toronto recently when a gentleman brought in a box of dental fillings to a precious metals dealer. The purpose of his visit was to sell the fillings for their gold content. The man was vague when asked where he got the fillings, but a suspicion was raised when he divulged his profession. No, he wasn't a dentist, he was an undertaker. (The chances are that the gold in your ring came from a Canadian mine—but then again, it may have come from Cleopatra's necklace.)

There are a number of ways to invest in gold and silver as an inflation hedge. Because of their volatility, both metals can also be useful for trading purposes, or short term speculation.

Let's start by ruling out jewellery. The mark-up in jewellery— whether it be gold, silver or precious stones—is so high that it will take a huge price move just to recoup your cost. When you sell jewellery, you will be paid *nothing* for the workmanship in the article. The gold or silver content (the intrinsic value) will be assessed, and that's what the price will be based upon. Because gold is so soft, it is usually alloyed with other metals such as copper or silver. The word "carat" preceded by a number e.g., "10 carat," describes the actual gold content. Pure gold contains 24 carats, thus a 10 carat item contains 10/24ths of pure gold; an 18 carat item 18/24ths and so on. Gold jewellery is nice to own, but it's a poor investment.

The same applies to rare gold coins. Here again you run into the problem of buying retail and selling wholesale. A large part of the cost of a rare coin is made up of its numismatic value rather than its intrinsic value. During periods of economic hardship the numismatic value shrinks to almost nothing. What counts is the gold content. If you doubt this statement, consider the number of coin dealers who went belly-up during the last recession.

Common gold coins, such as the one ounce Krugerrand or the Maple Leaf, have little numismatic value. This makes them an interesting investment. Although the Krugerrand is larger in diameter than the Maple Leaf, both contain exactly one ounce of gold. (The Canadian Maple Leaf is .9999 pure gold). Because they are recognized throughout the world, and represent the standard trading unit, these two coins have excellent marketability. They are convenient to own, attractive to look at, and take up little room under your mattress.

You can buy Krugerrands and Maple Leaf coins from many coin dealers, several Canadian banks, at least one trust company, and (would you believe it) Simpson-Sears. Prices vary widely among these outlets, and it will pay you to shop around before making a purchase. When you go through this exercise, write down all the figures and check to see if there are any additional charges. Some dealers offer gold coins in Canadian funds while other quote in American funds—this can make a hell of a difference. Also, there can be commission or handling charges added to the price (the Bank of Nova Scotia levies *both* on the purchase of coins). Sales tax is another thing to watch when buying coins. This varies from province to province, and can add dramatically to the cost. At this writing Quebec does not charge sales tax on coins, and by agreement none of the provinces charge tax on the Maple Leaf issues.

You may also wish to consider the purchase of gold or silver bullion, which is the refined metal in bar or wafer form. There is no sales tax on bullion. However, one problem with bullion is that you have to store it, or pay an institution to store it for you. When you sell bullion, unless you take it back to the vendor (with proof of purchase), you may have to pay for the metal to be assayed. Both these problems are eliminated if you buy a bullion *certificate*. This certificate gives you clear title to whatever quantity of gold or silver you have purchased, and the institution holds it in safekeeping for you. Several Canadian institutions including the Bank of Nova Scotia and Guardian Trust sell bullion certificates, and they can also be bought on the Montreal Exchange. Unless you are a dyed-in-the-wool gold bug, who must have the metal stashed in your bunker, this is the sensible way to buy bullion.

Before leaving the subject of coins and bullion, I must add that both are negative investments. The reason for this is that they provide no return on your money. In fact, it costs you money to hold them when you consider insurance and storage charges—not to mention the lost opportunity factor. Also, you must pay for coins and bullion in full, which eliminates leverage on your investment.

However, there are two highly leveraged ways you can play gold and silver. One is with futures, the other with options.

Gold futures are traded on the century-old Winnipeg Commodity Exchange and silver futures are traded on the Toronto Futures Exchange, but the best market for both gold and silver is the Comex in New York. On the Comex the contract size for gold is one hundred troy ounces. Thus a one dollar move in the price of gold means a hundred dollar change in the value of a contract. The size of the Comex silver contract is five thousand ounces. Therefore a one cent move in the price of silver changes the value of a contract by fifty dollars. Recently silver has been the most active of the precious metals on the Comex. Most people trade gold and silver futures for the short term, and try to catch the swings. This requires some agility, and a good dollop of luck.

Options on gold and silver are traded in Canada. The Montreal and Vancouver exchanges trade options on both metals, while the Toronto Stock Exchange (at this writing) only trades silver options and the Winnipeg Commodity exchange trades gold calls. The principles that apply to precious metal options are exactly the same as those for stock options. There is however, one important difference. All trades for gold and silver options are in U.S. dollars. Because of the volatility of these metals, the options and the Winnipeg Commodity Exchange trades gold calls. The principles that apply to precious metal options are Buy calls or puts, but do *not* write "naked calls," no matter how tempting the premium. It just isn't worth the risk.

The most popular way to invest in gold is to own shares in a mine. Canada is the third largest gold producer in the world, so there are hundreds of mines to choose from. If you are investing—as opposed to speculating—you should restrict your choice to mines that meet the following criteria:

1. Substantial *proven* ore reserves.
2. Low cost of production.
3. Relatively little debt.
4. Good management.

Ore reserves relate directly to the future life of the mine. It's no good buying a mine that is running out of ore. The cost of

production is critical because this determines the level of profitability. If it costs a mine $300 to produce an ounce of gold and
the prevailing price is $320, it will make a small profit. If the price
of gold falls below $300, the mine will lose money. The lower the
cost of production, the greater the cushion you have against a
decline in the price of gold. The amount of debt is also a factor
to consider. If interest rates soar, this can have a severe impact
on the profitability of the mine. Quality of management applies
to any business, and mines are no exception.

Here is a short list of investment quality gold mines that you
might consider. There's no point in trying to rate them in a
pecking order, because relative values are constantly changing.
If you are interested in comparing them and finding the best
buys, speak to your broker. This is by no means a definitive list,
but all the companies have good gold reserves, and some (like
Agnico-Eagle and Pegasus) also have silver:

Agnico-Eagle	Dome Mines	Kiena Gold
Bachelor Lake	Echo Bay	Lac Minerals
Campbell Red Lake	Giant Yellowknife	Pegasus
Dickenson Mines		

One of the most important gold discoveries in Canadian history is unfolding at Hemlo, in Northern Ontario. By the spring of
1984, drilling had indicated the presence of more than fourteen
million ounces of gold. The companies with the largest indicated
reserves in the Hemlo area are Lac Minerals, the partnership of
Noranda with Golden Sceptre and Goliath, Teck Corporation
and International Corona Resources.

The Hemlo discoveries have attracted tremendous interest in
the press. As a result of the publicity, stock promoters have had
a field day pushing companies whose only asset is property in
the vicinity of Hemlo. Most of these stock promotions originate
in Vancouver, and you would be well advised to avoid them.
(Penny dreadfuls will be discussed in more detail in the "Mines
& Oils" chapter.)

The shares of senior Canadian gold mines traditionally pay
small dividends and trade at relatively high multiples. Investors
buy these companies not for income, but for their wealth in the
ground. On the other hand, shares of South African gold mines

trade at relatively low multiples, and some pay handsome dividends. There are a number of reasons why South African gold shares do not command higher prices. Production costs in South Africa are rising steeply as a result of recent wage settlements. Some of the larger mines are running out of high grade ore, and are mining less profitable ore. These are important factors, but the main reason that South African gold shares are out of favour is the political risk. If racial tensions explode in South Africa, the mines could easily be shut down. This, in my opinion, eliminates them as a suitable investment.

One of the best strategies is to buy a "package" of Canadian gold mines. An easy way to do this is to purchase one of the four Closed-End gold funds that are listed on the Toronto Stock Exchange. For your guidance, here are the funds in alphabetical order:

> BGR Precious Metals
> Central Fund
> Goldcorp
> Guardian—Morton Shulman

Each of these funds has a different investment philosophy, so you should do some research before you commit yourself. Because they are Closed-End funds, they do *not* redeem their shares, and they normally trade at a *discount* to their net asset or break-up value. They also have share purchase warrants outstanding which will be of interest to aggressive investors.

To my mind, the warrants issued by Echo Bay have the most appeal. Echo Bay Mines Limited owns the Lupin mine at Contwoyto Lake in the North West Territories. It is a highly efficient gold mine with excellent ore reserves. Brought into production in October of 1982, the Lupin mine in 1983 was the third largest gold producer in Canada. When Echo Bay preferred shares were underwritten in 1981, each share was sold as a unit with four gold purchase warrants. The warrants have since been detached and are now listed on the Toronto Stock Exchange. The warrants expire in four successive years, from 1986 to 1989.

So much for the background, now let's get to the interesting part. Each Echo Bay warrant entitles the holder to buy 0.01765 of an ounce of gold at $5.25US. Thus to acquire one ounce of gold you need fifty-seven warrants, plus $297.50US in cash. Upon maturity of the warrant (in 1986, 1987, 1988, or 1989) you can elect to take the cash equivalent of an ounce of gold rather than bullion. *The warrants also have a "put" feature.* If the price of gold is less than $595 US when your warrant matures, you can "put" your warrant to the company for a price of $5.25 in U.S. funds.

You may have to read over the terms again, to fully understand them, because these warrants are unique. The fact that they are difficult to understand has caused many investors to shy away from them. This has tended to keep their prices *below* the amount (in Canadian dollars, at present rate of exchange) you can receive from the company if the price of gold is less than $595 US at maturity. When this is the case you have the stock market play off the warrant, but if gold doesn't perform, you can get your money back! Not only can you speculate on a price rise in the value of the warrants, but you can also lock in the purchase of gold at a fixed price. Your only risks are that Echo Bay will not be able to produce the gold, or be unable to pay for the redemption of the warrants. As the company has large ore reserves and a strong balance sheet, these risks are remote.

What is the outlook for gold? Nobody knows the answer to this question. Some people believe that gold has had its day, and it will eventually settle around the two hundred dollar level. Others, and this includes experts like the Aden sisters (who run an advisory service from Puerto Rico) predict that during the next three to five years gold will exceed three thousand dollars an ounce.

When should you sell your gold? Let me tell you of a personal experience. When gold started its meteoric rise in the autumn of 1979, I thought it was just a flash in the pan. I continued to hold this view during the next few months and did not buy any gold. I was confident that the price would soon fall. However, gold kept on going up and every morning the announcer on the C.B.C. news would tell me of the latest hike in price. This worked like a Chinese water torture, because I was constantly reminded of what I was missing. Finally, I capitulated and decided to make a token purchase of ten ounces of gold. This I reasoned, would give me peace of mind. The price of gold at that time was around $730 and silver was around $29 an ounce.

I went to the Bank of Nova Scotia bright and early, but there was a long line-up to buy gold and silver. In fact, I had to get a ticket with a number, like you do in a crowded bakery. As I stood in line I couldn't help overhearing some nearby conversations. Everyone it seemed was buying, and no one in the line had ever invested before. This got me to thinking. Gold had taken a long and dramatic run-up in price, and people were now so anxious to buy it that they were gambling with the grocery money. When this sunk in, I realized that I was being an absolute fool. I gave my ticket to the woman standing behind me, and fled from the bank. Gold continued up for a few more weeks, and then the bottom fell out of the market.

The moral of this story is that after gold has had a prolonged rise, and you see people lining up to buy it—that's the time to sell.

CHAPTER 12

High Tech Stocks

HIGH TECH STOCKS are like the little girl with the curl in the centre of her forehead. When they are good they are very, very good, but when they are bad they are horrid. I know people in Ottawa who have literally made millions from high tech investments. Without exception, all of these people held shares in companies *before* they went public. However, the experience of investors who bought high tech stocks *after* they were issued has been quite different. Some have made good profits, but many have lost money. For this reason you should approach high tech stocks the same way that porcupines make love—with great care.

The term "high tech" refers to companies that sell products or services of an advanced technological nature. The high tech spectrum includes companies engaged in electronics, robotics, communications, biotechnology, lasers, and other scientific areas. Computers form the core of the high tech industry.

The computer field is divided into two main sectors: computer hardware and computer software. Computer hardware is the machinery that processes software. As a crude analogy hardware may be likened to a record player and software to the records that are played on it. Today, hardware manufacturers are faced with a crowded market and widespread discounting of prices. As an example, micro computers retail from two to seven thousand dollars, but a bright seventeen-year-old can buy the components and make himself an acceptable micro for five hundred dollars. From an investment point of view, shares of software manufacturers currently offer the best potential.

Although many technology companies have suffered severe reverses, the industry as a whole has enjoyed a phenomenal growth rate. This growth is expected to continue because we are in the midst of the technological revolution. I see it in my office, where I use a computer terminal to retrieve market information on a video screen. This arrangement is infinitely better than the old system. I also see it in my home, where I write on a word processor which is far more efficient than my old electric typewriter. What the technological revolution means to you is that there will be all sorts of investment opportunities in the future.

The technological revolution started in Canada more than twenty years ago. I first invested in a high tech stock around 1968. The company was called International Systcoms, and it had invented a briefcase telephone which at that time was an exciting breakthrough. The shares of Systcoms were unlisted, and the market for the stock was being run by a brokerage firm in Montreal. I got involved in the stock through one of my clients who was connected with the company. Because Systcoms was believed to have limitless potential it captured the imagination of the public. As a result, the shares took off like a blue-assed fly. I was in and out of the stock quite often, and I remember one particular day when I bought some shares just before I went to lunch. On my return, I found that I was up seven thousand dollars on my purchase. It seemed such an easy way to make money.

Systcoms stock went from about two dollars to forty dollars in a matter of months. Then, for no apparent reason, the price started to decline. I checked with my contact who assured me all was well with the company. Armed with this inside information, I bought two thousand shares at twenty-three dollars, which I thought was a bargain price.

Shortly after buying these shares I left for a trip to the North. The first thing I did when I returned to civilization was to phone my office in Ottawa. The call was made from a phone booth on the edge of the tarmac at Val d'Or airport, a few hundred feet from the plane. When I asked about the price of Systcoms there was an ominous pause and then my colleague replied in a funereal voice: "Seven dollars a share." I immediately told him to sell my shares. On the way back to the plane (an old DC 3) I nearly walked into the propellers.

Systcoms was what is known as a "concept" stock. When you buy a concept stock you are buying the sizzle, not the steak. Systcoms never did work out the way we had hoped, nor did the stock recover. The company was later reorganized, given a new name, and the stock underwent a reverse split. The only smart move I made was to take my loss quickly. When I last checked, the shares I sold for seven dollars were trading at fifteen cents.

After the Systcoms escapade, I decided that the next time I got into a concept stock it would be on the ground floor. The following year I joined a syndicate who bought founding shares in a hovercraft company. (A hovercraft is an all-terrain vehicle that travels on a cushion of air.) Our hovercraft was designed for personal use, and it was meant to retail for less than the price of a car. We thought it would appeal to a gigantic market. Unfortunately, we never found out because none were sold. The prototype machines had recurring flaws, and before they were solved the company went bankrupt. It was an expensive learning experience, and I still wince when I hear the word "hovercraft."

This misadventure taught me that early investors have the greatest potential for gain, but they can also lose their *entire* investment. In this connection, fledgling companies invariably need *more time and more money* than you think. With this in mind, I determined that I would be more careful in the future—and I would avoid concept stocks.

Around 1970 I was one of a group of private investors who helped finance a word processing company called Alphatext Limited. This was a soundly conceived enterprise that had firm contracts for its data retrieval and word processing services. Among its financial backers were members of the Steinberg family from Montreal and a major oil company. Alphatext functioned for many years before it was taken over by another company. Sadly, it never seemed to make any money. At least not for the shareholders. When I finally sold my stock, I took a sizeable loss.

I recount these experiences to show that I have paid my entrance fee into the high tech game, and to illustrate some of its pitfalls.

But for those who are smart (or lucky) the game can be incredibly rewarding. A young Ottawa lawyer invested between fifteen and twenty thousand dollars in Mitel when it was in its infancy. In return for his money he received common shares in the company. Several years later Mitel went public, and the common shares were split. In 1981, when Mitel stock reached its peak, this fellow's investment of less than twenty thousand dollars was worth more than twenty-five million dollars.

For every successful high tech company, there are at least twenty that fail. Probably more. To understand how this happens, let's go through the genesis and development of a typical company in the field.

Usually it is founded by one or two highly qualified persons who work for one of the giants such as IBM, Xerox, or Northern Telecom. The founders are well paid employees with a secure future, but they have a deep-seated ambition to be out on their own. Eventually, they resign from the firm and start their own company. To get the company going they pool their savings, mortgage their houses, and work eighteen hours a day. If they are fortunate, they produce a product or a service that is bought by another high tech company or by a government agency. (If they don't produce a commercial product, the company fails.) The company's first big sale usually precipitates a financial crisis, because money must be raised to finance the contract. It is at this point that they turn to the bank or to private investors. (Here again, if the company can't get money from either source it will fold.)

To fill the contract the company will probably have to expand its premises and hire several employees. This is usually the first tangible evidence of growth. If the customer is satisfied, other contracts will follow. Success invariably produces more financial crises due to the "upfront" costs associated with the new orders. If money is forthcoming, it will usually be from private investors who buy treasury shares. (Banks are reluctant to lend money to struggling small businesses—no matter how bright the prospects.)

Up to this stage the founders have personally attended to every aspect of the company's operations, including research, production, marketing, and finance. Assuming the firm can sustain a high rate of growth for three to five years, the founders may be approached by an investment dealer to discuss a share underwriting. There are two basic reasons for selling treasury shares to the public. The first is to raise money for the company so that it can eliminate its debt and/or pay for further expansion. The second—and this does not happen in every case—is to sell some of the founders' and private investors' shares so that they can realize a return on their investment.

The price of the shares to the public is *always* as high as the traffic will bear. Often it is difficult to tell whether the shares are fairly priced. You can't judge a high tech issue on its Net Asset Value, because its most valuable assets walk out of the door every night at five o'clock. A better yardstick to use is the Price/ Earnings ratio of the stock. What's a reasonable Price/Earnings ratio? There's no pat answer to this question, but I wouldn't pay more than twenty times earnings for *any* new issue. (And for a listed issue with a proven growth rate, I wouldn't pay more than twenty times *next year's* estimated earnings.) It is unlikely that a new issue will pay a dividend, because earnings are normally reinvested in the company. In recent years, new high tech issues have had a mixed reception, and a fair number have settled *below* their original offering price.

After the shares of a high tech company are listed, they will trade on the basis of *future expectations* rather than on past performance. This means the price will be determined more by emotion than by logic. If a company can put together a string of good quarterly reports, the shares can easily soar to a ridiculous multiple. But public sentiment can change in an instant. Should the same company publish a poor report, the market may react viciously to the news. Because of the emotional factor and the volatility of earnings, high tech stocks are subject to wide swings in price. As a result, timing is critical when buying or selling them.

If you are trying to pick a promising high tech stock, what should you look for? I had lunch the other day with Doug Cameron, the president of Noranda Enterprises Limited, and asked him this question. Noranda Enterprises, the technology investment arm of Noranda Mines, was started by Maclaren Power & Paper in 1973. It is probably the largest high tech investor in Canada, and it has been phenomenally successful. The policy of Noranda Enterprises is to buy at least twenty per cent of the equity of an emerging high tech company, and to hold this investment for the long term. The size of Noranda Enterprises's portfolio is a secret, but an educated guess would place it at more than one hundred million dollars.

Doug Cameron told me that he looks for the following characteristics in a high tech company:

1. The first and most essential thing is the *quality of management*. The company must have a management team that is exceptionally skilled, highly motivated, and concerned with making a *profit*.

2. The company must have *innovative or proprietary technology* that is difficult for competitors to imitate.

3. The *market* for the product or technology should be *large, well developed, international* in scope, and offer the promise of *long term growth*. (Ideally, there should be a technology barrier that will allow the company to establish itself before competition enters the market.)

4. *Research and Development* must be carefully controlled and directed towards *improving the product* line. (This eliminates speculative or pure research.)

5. The company must have a sound *long term game plan*.

These are guidelines for investment in emerging high tech companies, but they also apply to mature companies. Indeed, when I asked the senior high tech analyst in my firm what he looked for in these stocks, his list was almost identical.

You will notice—and it may surprise you—that it is not the product, but management that is the most essential thing. This is true of any business, and high tech companies are no exception. Poor management is the reason that a number of Canadian high tech companies have recently run aground. There is no need to cite examples, just look at the stocks that have fallen the most, and then check their earnings. In every case, top management is responsible for the poor results.

To end this chapter on a positive note, let me mention three Canadian high tech companies that are considered by industry observers to have excellent management:

Northern Telecom Limited—Founded in 1914, Northern Telecom is Canada's largest designer and manufacturer of communications equipment. It has forty-six manufacturing plants around the world and annual revenues of more than four billion dollars. The shares are listed on the Toronto, Montreal, Vancouver, and New York stock exchanges, and you can also trade options on the stock.

Lumonics Inc.—Founded in 1970, Lumonics designs and manufactures a wide variety of lasers for industrial, scientific, and medical use. Lumonics laser applications range from marking Coke bottles to cutting steel and performing delicate eye surgery. It is the only Canadian laser company whose shares (listed in Toronto) are available to the public. Earnings have increased every year for the past twelve years.

Geac Computer Corporation Limited—Founded in 1971, Geac designs and manufactures proprietary computer hardware and software. These systems, which service many terminals and access large databases, are particularly useful to libraries and financial institutions. Geac's success in penetrating these markets has solidly established the company in the high tech field. Its shares are listed on the Toronto Stock Exchange.

Finally, for those of you who consider high tech stocks too risky, I have a suggestion. Why not buy some shares in Bell Enterprises? Bell owns fifty-five per cent of Northern Telecom, which is regarded by some analysts as the finest communications company in the world. Bell shares are not prone to violent fluctuations, they trade at a low Price/Earnings ratio, and they pay a big dividend. If you buy Bell you can sleep soundly at night, enjoy a good income—and still participate in the high tech revolution.

CHAPTER 13

Mines & Oils

ONE DEFINITION of a mine is a hole in the ground with a liar standing at the top. This is a fair description of many junior resource plays, but established mining and oil companies are sound investments. For years International Nickel was considered the bluest of Canada's blue chips, and the largest corporation in North America is not General Motors, but Exxon—an oil company.

Let's start at the bottom, with speculative mines. Many of Canada's major mines came into existence because someone was willing to take a gamble. In the old days, the gamble might be taken by a storekeeper who extended credit to a prospector on the understanding that if the prospector found anything, the storekeeper would share in the discovery. This practice was known as "grubstaking." Today, very few prospectors like Ben Hollinger or Sandy McIntyre lurch off into the wilderness with a pack on their back looking for the Mother Lode. Prospecting is done by companies, and the person who grubstakes them is often a mining promoter.

This may suggest that mining promoters are an altruistic lot, who risk their own money to increase Canada's mineral wealth. Sometimes they do risk their own money, but they prefer to risk yours, and the object of the exercise is to enhance their own account. To understand the junior mining game it is useful to know how promoters operate, because promoters are behind most of the speculative plays.

There are several ways to promote a mining stock. Regardless of the method used, the aim of a promotion is to increase the price of the shares by giving them a "run." A stock that is given a run without subsequent financing serves no useful purpose other than to line the pockets of the promoter and his friends.

On the positive side, a promotion can raise money for a company through the sale of treasury shares, and this money can finance the exploration or development of a property. Were it not for promoters, the flow of risk capital for speculative ventures would dry up to a trickle and Canada's resource industries would suffer.

A typical mining promotion unfolds over a period of months, or even years, and is planned with great care. First, the promoter buys control of an inactive or dormant company. He then sells the company some mining claims and is paid in treasury shares. Now the promoter has control of the company and a substantial block of stock at a token price. Because there are escrow rules (which mean that treasury shares can't be sold for a number of months) the promoter bides his time.

When the promoters' shares are out of escrow, he alerts the public that his company is about to drill on the newly acquired property. His publicity campaign is orchestrated through telephone contacts around the country. If he is a big operator, these contacts will not only include brokers and other influential people in Canada, but also in the United States, and possibly in Europe. As a result of the promotion, the stock becomes active on the exchange and the price begins to move up—although nothing has happened on the property.

Having created public interest and a gratifying move in the stock, the next step is to sell the public some shares from the treasury. If the promotion is handled with finesse, the shares will be snapped up by eager buyers. Barely half of the money raised by the underwriting ends up in the treasury; the rest is siphoned off by the promoter for services rendered or used to pay brokerage fees. The net proceeds, however, are usually sufficient to finance a drilling program. Now the promotion moves into high gear, and the stock really takes off.

The period between the announcement of a drilling program and the announcement of the results is when the promoter makes hay. Anticipation, fueled by extravagant rumours, can cause a speculative mining stock to soar. Usually the promoter sells most of his shares into this euphoric market. He now has all his money back and a handsome profit. Should the drilling prove unsuccessful (and unless you are an insider you won't know until it's too late) the stock collapses. If the drilling is successful, that's a surprising bonus.

Variations of the promotional cycle are repeated over and over again. I mention it to you so that you can recognize the pattern and act accordingly. *Most people lose money because they buy too late in the cycle, and hold their shares until the bitter end.* The best way to play a promotion is to buy early and to ride the wave of anticipation. But don't wait around for the big payoff, sell your stock *before* the results are known and be content with a reasonable profit.

I should add that not all mining plays are promotions. There are plenty of small companies run by honest people who are trying to find a commercial orebody, and there are also junior companies with proven reserves that are struggling to raise funds to go into production. Because the shares of these companies are not manipulated, they attract less attention than promoted stocks.

For years most of the stock promoters were based in Toronto, and the Toronto Stock Exchange had the lion's share of specula- tive listings. However, the Windfall Scandal in 1964 and the Royal Commission that followed in its wake forced Toronto to clean up its act. As a result, most of the promoters moved to Vancouver.

Viola MacMillan was the promoter behind Windfall Oils and Mines. A tough and energetic woman, Viola was nicknamed the Queen Bee of Mining and the Petticoat Prospector. For more than twenty years she was also the respected president of the Prospectors and Developers Association. After the sensational base metal strike at Kidd Creek near Timmins by Texas Gulf in 1963, Viola acquired a piece of property for Windfall Oils and Mines adjacent to the Kidd Creed discovery. Drilling was done on the claims but no commercial ore was found. Despite this fact, the shares of Windfall were given an incredible run before the truth came out and the price of the shares collapsed. Viola was subsequently found guilty of stock manipulation, and served a short sentence in the slammer.

After the promoters moved west, the Vancouver Stock Exchange became the busiest market for junior resource stocks in North America. This free-wheeling market, combined with British Columbia's lenient securities regulations, make Vancouver a stock promoter's paradise. If you're a speculator, and you're looking for action, you'll find it on the Vancouver Exchange. I need hardly mention that you'll be playing in fast company, and the odds are five to one that you'll lose.

The gaudiest rooster in the Vancouver financial barnyard is a gentleman by the name of Murray Pezim. To friend and foe he is known as "The Pez" and he is fond of describing himself as "the greatest mining promoter that ever lived." Pezim learned the business in Toronto and came to Vancouver in the Sixties. During his checkered career he has made and lost fortunes, he has been tried and acquitted on charges of fraud, and on at least one occasion he has had to declare personal bankruptcy. Today, he has a string of fifty or sixty companies and measures his worth in tens of millions. What sets him apart from his colleagues, and eases the pain of his followers, is his willingness to risk his own money in some of his promotions. Many of his deals have caused catastrophic losses, but a few have resulted in valuable discoveries. (The most notable being International Corona Resources, the first company to make a major gold strike in the Hemlo area.) The Pez is famous for his ability to move a stock— but before you board one of his high fliers, it would be wise to strap on a parachute. You may need it.

When speculating on a junior mine there are certain things you should check before making the plunge. First, the stock must be listed, if it's not listed forget it. Next, find out who controls the company. You want people with integrity and a record of success. What does the company hope to find? If the company has a hot uranium prospect, this will not whip up much enthusiasm, although it would have thirty years ago. (The

Pez got his start in the uranium boom of the 1950s'.) The company must be looking for a metal that is currently in strong demand, such as gold, silver, or copper.

Now look at the company's balance sheet. How many shares are outstanding? A company with three million shares is obviously more attractive than one with thirty million, because the fewer the shares the greater the impact of a discovery. In this connection, you should also estimate the "float" which is the number of shares in the hands of the public. Many companies are controlled by a family or a syndicate—this control block can be *deducted* from the total because it will not be traded. If a stock has a small float, it will take relatively little buying to move it up in price. When looking at the capitalization, check if there are warrants outstanding. The exercise of warrants will dilute the value of the existing common shares. By the same token, if there are escrowed shares, you should find out when they will be released from escrow (and possibly dumped on the market).

On the financial side, note how much money is in the treasury. Is it enough to finance a comprehensive drilling program? If not, there will probably be an underwriting which would dilute the value of your stock.

The price of the shares is also a consideration. If the shares are trading near the top of their range for the past year, they may be in the terminal phase of a promotional cycle. This is a tough one to call. Ideally, you should buy shares in the lower portion of their previous twelve month range.

Having done this preliminary investigation, you can now look at the mining aspects of the deal. The location of the discovery (or prospect) is of prime importance. Is it near to a proven orebody? If the answer is yes, this will improve the odds but is *no guarantee of success*. Many worthless stocks are touted on the basis of claims that are near a major orebody. The Hemlo area is the current favourite for this type of promotion. As a digression, promoters like to imply that there is certain to be ore on the property because a survey has revealed a huge "anomoly." An anomoly is merely an aberration in the geophysical survey (rather like a shadow on an X-Ray), and very few anomolies indicate an orebody. In fact, one of the old jokes in the mining game is that the way to ruin a good anomoly is to drill it.

Getting back to the location, how remote is it? If it is far from civilization it might not be feasible to bring a mine into production because of the cost of the infrastructure (building a road, camp site etc.). The only exception would be a gigantic discovery—such as the Echo Bay gold mine, which is fifty miles from the Arctic Circle.

If it's a drilling play, how many holes are they going to drill? You don't want to gamble on just a few holes. From a market standpoint, an extensive drilling program can be very good for the stock, particularly if one of the early holes has encouraging results. Promoters love this type of situation because speculative fever mounts with each succeeding hole.

If drilling has commenced, don't buy the stock on the basis of a single hole. A lucky hole can produce totally misleading results. Wait for a "step out" hole or some "fill-in" drilling. (A "step out" is a hole some distance away, and "fill-in" drilling is a series of holes close to the original one—both of which will provide more accurate information.) One drill hole doesn't make a mine any more than one swallow makes a summer.

To understand drill results you should realize that a drill hole is a blind probe, rather like a hollow needle pushed into a cake. The material in the core of the drill is brought to the surface and assayed for its mineral content. Many speculators get blinded by the grade of the ore. This is stupid because ore grade is meaningless if you don't take into account the *width and the length* of the intersection. I am not a geologist, but I know that the *true* width should be at least six feet (so that the ore can be mined) and the length of the intersection should be at least two hundred feet (to assure a commercial quantity of ore). Assuming that these requirements are met—and I am deliberately excluding low grade, high tonnage deposits—what are "boasting" grades of ore? I should mention here that base metal assays are normally given as a percentage while precious metal assays are usually stated in Troy ounces. From a *stock market point of view*, taking gold, silver, and copper as examples, the core should contain .5 ounces of gold per ton: 200 ounces of silver per ton: or 4% copper per ton.

Once an orebody has been outlined by a series of drill holes and the ore has been graded, there are still many questions to be answered. The basic one is whether it's a commercial discovery. All sorts of things must be considered—including the depth of the deposit, the rock structure, and the presence of other substances in the ore—before this can be determined. The bottom line is the cost of production. If you have a potential gold mine, and the cost to produce gold will be five hundred dollars US per ounce, it wouldn't be feasible to bring the property into production unless you were confident that gold was going to stay above five hundred dollars US an ounce. Another consideration is the environmental factor. Will the mine cause environmental problems—such as pollution of a river or a lake? After negotiating these and other obstacles there remains the question of financing, which can take years to solve. I mention these problems because many people think that once you've discovered an orebody you're home free. As you can see, this is far from the case.

Should you be lucky enough to buy the shares of a company that finds an orebody and subsequently goes into production, you may be surprised at the behaviour of your shares. They won't go straight up. The price will rise during the discovery period, settle back after the news is released, move up briefly on the production announcement, and then slump again until a few months before production actually begins. Here is a diagram that shows the typical pattern:

Established mines are quite different from speculative mines. The obvious difference is that many established mines earn large sums of money, and are considered quality investments. Producing mines are subject to three main influences: the economic cycle, metal prices, and the state of the general stock market. These cross currents cause wide swings in the price of their shares. For this reason you shouldn't buy senior mines and forget them. You should play the swings, buying them when they're cheap and selling them when they're dear. Sounds obvious, but to do it successfully requires exquisite timing.

First, you have to find where the mines are in the economic cycle. There are three distinct phases to watch for. At the end of a recession, mining shares (along with most other stocks) are bumping along the bottom. As soon as the stock market turns, prices of the senior mines move up with it, even though earnings may be non-existent. This is known as the Anticipation Phase. Following this surge, mining shares usually give up a third to a half of their gain. The next upward leg comes as a result of a recovery in their earnings and is known as the Fundamental Phase. Again, there is a substantial correction. The last and most exuberant move occurs at the end of the economic cycle, and is called the Speculative Phase. There is no recovery from this one —the mines go into a prolonged decline. The time to buy is at the beginning of the Anticipation or the Fundamental Phases, and the time to sell is during the Speculative Phase. This is what the three phases look like on a diagram:

THE MINING CYCLE

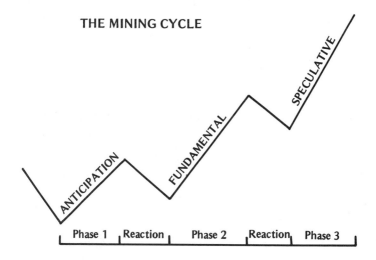

Having identified the stage of the economic cycle, your next task is to decide what metal you should play. Ask your broker for a research report on the outlook for metals, check the commodity quotes, and use your own common sense. For example, if the outlook for copper is good and the price of copper is rising, you might consider a copper stock. If auto production is increasing, take a look at lead and zinc stocks. The auto industry uses a lot of zinc (for galvanizing), and lead is used for car batteries. The auto industry also consumes a substantial amount of aluminum. If the economy is in a strong recovery and capital spending is on the rise, the steel companies will be busy. This is good for molybdenum and nickel, both of which are used as alloys in specialty steels.

After you have chosen a metal, look at the mines that produce that metal as their primary source of income. (Most mines also produce other metals as a by-product in the recovery process.) You can apply the normal yardsticks to pick a particular stock within the group. The Price/Earnings ratio is an obvious consideration. You should also check on the cost of production and the production per share. To find the production per share, divide the number of shares outstanding into the total amount of metal produced. For example, if a company has one million shares outstanding and it produces ten million pounds of copper in a year, the production per share will be ten pounds. The cost of production varies from company to company. Those with a low cost operation are much safer investments, but an increase in price of the metal provides little earnings leverage. On the other hand, a mine with a high cost of production is a riskier investment because of its break-even point, but a small increase in the metal price can make a dramatic difference to its earnings. Using gold as an example, here's how metal price leverage works:

Cost of Production	Gold Price (per ounce)	Effect of $10 Increase
Mine "A" $125	$400	3.6%
Mine "B" $380	$400	50.0%

Ore reserves—how much metal is left in the ground—relate

directly to the life expectancy of the mine. You want at least five or six years of reserves, although ore reserves can be deceptive. Some gold mines have gone on for decades reporting only two or three years reserves, but in the process of mining have found more ore each year.

Producing mines—unless the ore is running out—normally pay small dividends, and sell at relatively high Price/Earnings ratios. In "normal" years the average price is about seven to eight times annual earnings. Investors are willing to pay these prices and to accept low yields because mines are a good inflation hedge due to the fact that they have wealth in the ground. This is especially true of producing gold mines. The senior gold stocks sell at around twenty times earnings, or about twice as much as the average multiple of all other stocks. I can't remember when the shares of gold producers were "cheap," they always seem to be overpriced in relation to other mining stocks. Campbell Red Lake, which can produce gold at a cost of around $125 US an ounce, is a prime example.

Before leaving the mines, let me offer one more word of advice. If you're considering several mining stocks and you're not sure which one to choose—buy quality.

Now let's turn to oil stocks. Oil stocks are similar to mining stocks in that both are natural resource investments. They are also similar from a market point of view because drilling for oil has the same speculative potential as drilling for gold. Indeed, if it looks profitable, mining promoters will turn their hand to an oil play without batting an eye.

This reminds me of an oil stock listed on the Vancouver Exchange called Bata Resources that Murray Pezim promoted some years ago. It was a truly glorious promotion with all the right ingredients—a lengthy drilling program, several corporate mergers, and participation by an all-star international cast. With the skill of a conductor Pezim promoted Bata towards a magnificent crescendo. The performance lasted many months.

Bata was a company with genuine merit. I bought the stock for my own account at about three dollars and took several more bites up to six dollars, which gave me an average price of around five dollars per share. Bata worked its way up to thirteen dollars but then ran into heavy weather and started down again. Being tuned into the promotional network, I tried to find out if there were any serious problems. I heard from The Pez (second hand) that all was well, and if I was smart I should double up my position. Being a simple lad with a low threshold of pain, I did not heed his advice but sold my stock for nine dollars per share.

Bata shot up after I sold it, faltered, and then began a long descent. As the slide continued it became obvious that the promotion was losing its momentum. At this juncture the "pros" started shorting Bata. Pezim marshalled all the buying power he could, and poured in his own money to stave off these attacks, but it was a losing battle. The end for Bata came one fateful day in 1971 when the shorts broke the stock from three dollars to thirty cents.

The Pez suffered grievous loss on this venture, as did his followers, including a friend of mine who lost over $100,000 after being up more than $800,000. Among the other casualties was a brokerage firm in California that went down the drain.

As a general rule, oil promotions are just as dangerous as mining promotions, and they can contain the same elements of chicanery. If you are going to gamble on an oil play you should screen it as carefully as a mining speculation. The most important thing to find out is the integrity and track record of the people behind the deal. If they're honest, and they've been successful in the past, you'll probably get a fair shake for your money.

The oil and gas situation in Canada is rather peculiar and I'll try to summarize it briefly. Canada has massive natural gas reserves and a good supply of oil. Most of the country's natural gas comes from the Prairie provinces and most of the oil from Alberta. Natural gas reserves are sufficient to last for many years, and are large enough to justify sales to other countries (primarily the United States). The oil picture is not as bright because Canada has to import a certain amount of oil. As a result of the National Energy Policy—which was designed to conserve our oil and gas supply, and to make the country self sufficient—production and prices for domestic oil and gas are regulated by the federal and provincial governments.

Because natural gas is sold on a contract basis, many natural gas wells are capped. Capped wells represent wealth in the ground for a company, but don't produce any income until a contract is obtained. The production of oil is also regulated and subject to two different prices. Oil discovered before 1 April 1974 is subject to Conventional Old Oil Prices (COOP) which means that it can be sold for approximately seventy-five per cent of the world price. Oil discovered after 1 April 1974 (and oil from enhanced recovery and experimental schemes) qualifies for NORP, the New Oil Reference Price. The price of NORP oil is computed by a formula that gives roughly the equivalent of the world price. Therefore, companies with a substantial percentage of "new" oil make a higher profit than those whose production is mainly from "old" oil. The government's reason for the two prices is to encourage exploration.

Petroleum Incentive Payments are also made by the government to encourage exploration. These payments (known as PIP grants), are higher for Canadian companies than for foreign companies, and can cover as much as eighty per cent of the cost of a frontier exploration project. To qualify as a Canadian company for a PIP grant at least half of the voting shares must be owned by Canadians.

The market for oil stocks has been dampened by the recent recession, a glut of natural gas in North America, and a lower world price for oil. Nevertheless, there are good opportunities for profit in the junior sector.

I'm not referring to the penny dreadfuls, but to small producing companies. What you should look for are Canadian firms that survived the recession with a healthy balance sheet. This indicates good management. Don't rely on Net Asset Values (which can be suspect) or compare earnings, but look at the *cash flow* of these companies. (Cash flow is the sum of net income plus deferred taxes plus non-cash charges such as amortization, depreciation, and depletion). Cash flow is important because it shows what funds are available for future exploration. To create market interest the exploration program should include a number of low risk plays in Western Canada—which will provide encouraging news—and a high risk frontier play for a speculative boost. It might also have a participation in an overseas drilling play. Junior stocks with this profile should be excellent performers over the next few years.

Don't get carried away by the discovery of a major oil well in Indonesia or some other far-off place (except for Australia or the North Sea). The reason I caution you is that no matter how sensational the find, it will be vulnerable to both political and war risks. An obvious political risk is the government of the host country arbitrarily confiscating the oil well. A war risk could be an Exocet missile instantaneously erasing the well. In either case, there's nothing the company can do about it. For this reason, oil and gas discoveries on the North American continent are far more valuable than those overseas.

The heavyweights in the oil and gas industry are the integrated oils, such as Imperial, Gulf, and Texaco. The term "integrated" refers to vertical integration, meaning that they do everything from exploration to the sale of the refined product at the gas pump. The most profitable part of their business comes from the "upstream" end rather than the "downstream" end. ("Upstream" is the production of oil, "downstream" is the refining and marketing of it.) Because of the fundamental change in oil and gas consumption that has taken place in the last decade, the integrated companies expect little growth in the downstream end. However, the production side of their business is expected to be good for the forseeable future.

The senior integrated oils are sound and conservative investments. They trade on an earnings basis the same as industrial stocks. A reasonable price for an integrated oil stock would be around ten times earnings, with a yield of about three per cent. The reason for the modest yield is that oil companies reinvest a substantial amount of their earnings in exploration and development. Gulf Canada, because of its frontier exploration program, is my favourite among the senior oils.

As an investor I would recommend that you have some Canadian oil and gas shares in your portfolio. The juniors, including those with shut-in natural gas, will do well for a number of reasons. Looking down the road, it is certain that the demand for natural gas will pick up. The outlook for oil—despite its high price and conservation programs—is also good. After all, oil is energy, and energy will always be in demand.

CHAPTER 14

RRSPs &
Other Tax Shelters

DEATH AND TAXES are unavoidable. You can do nothing about the former, but you can take steps to reduce the amount of tax you pay. The purpose of this chapter is to outline in broad strokes some of the legitimate ways you can ease the tax bite.

At the outset I would like to stress that for tax advice you should consult an accountant or a tax lawyer—not your banker, trust company manager, mutual fund salesperson, or broker. And don't be put off by the belief that tax experts are just for the very rich. I've used an accountant for years, and have found that the tax savings far outweigh the cost of his fees.

To understand how tax savings can help you, we should first review how personal taxes are levied in Canada. Personal income tax is levied by both the federal and the provincial governments. The federal tax is the same for all Canadians, but the provincial rates and methods of taxation vary from province to province.

To compute your personal tax you begin by totalling your earnings and income from all sources to get your "Gross Income." You then subtract all your allowable deductions and exemptions from your Gross Income. This gives you your "Taxable Income." Federal tax is calculated on the basis of your Taxable Income, and the amount payable is reduced by any

Canadian dividend or Research and Development tax credits. Having calculated your tax and made these deductions the amount left is your "Basic Federal Tax." (This figure can then be further reduced by certain witholding taxes paid on foreign investments and by the special two hundred dollar federal tax credit.) Here is a simplified version of the steps:

Gross Income minus exemptions and deductions = *Taxable Income*
Calculate Federal Tax on Taxable Income
Deduct from this figure Canadian dividend and R & D Tax Credits
Net amount = *Basic Federal Tax.*

Your Basic Federal Tax is important because it is the figure used to calculate your provincial tax. All the provinces, except for Quebec, levy their tax as a fixed percentage of the Basic Federal Tax (and some of the provinces also levy surcharges). Quebec residents only pay 83.5% of the Basic Federal Tax, but this is an illusory benefit because Quebec then socks the individual with a hefty provincial tax.

You can see from the foregoing that the higher your Basic Federal Tax, the more you will pay to both the federal government and your provincial government. For this reason, the name of the game is to lower your Basic Federal Tax. This can be done in one of two ways—or a combination of both—by reducing your Taxable Income (through deductions) or by increasing your Tax Credits.

Now that we've identified the target—Basic Federal Tax—let's look at some of the ways investors can reduce it to a less onerous size.

Investment income is treated in several ways. Interest from bonds, savings accounts, Guaranteed Investment Certificates, mortgages etc., must be reported in full. Income from foreign investments is treated the same way , except that in some cases witholding tax deducted at source can be deducted from Basic Federal Tax.

Dividend income from Canadian companies is quite different. The income from Canadian dividends is overstated by being "grossed-up" by fifty per cent, (which inflates your Taxable Income) but you are then allowed to deduct thirty-four per cent of the *actual* dividends from your tax calculation to arrive at your Basic Federal Tax. The effect of the tax credit is to give you an after tax return of roughly *one and a half times the amount you would receive from an equal amount of interest income.* Here is an example showing the advantage of dividend income over interest income. In this case the investor is in the thirty per cent federal tax bracket, and lives in a province with a fifty per cent tax rate:

	Dividends	**Interest**
Amount of income	$1000	$1000
50% gross-up	500	n/a
Taxable Income	$1500	$1000
Federal Tax @ 30%	450	300
34% Tax Credit	– 340	n/a
Basic Federal Tax	$ 110	$ 300
Provincial tax @ 50%	+ 55	+ 150
Total tax	$ 165	$ 450
Net After-tax income	$ 835	$ 550

The dividend tax credit is a boon to investors in every tax bracket. In all of the provinces, except Quebec, if your sole source of income is Canadian dividends, you can have a Gross Income of more than $35,000 and—after taking your standard deductions and exemptions, including the Investment Income Deduction—you will pay nothing in tax!

The Investment Income Deduction applies to everyone and allows you to deduct a maximum of one thousand dollars from certain types of interest, dividends, and capital gains. Therefore, this deduction means that you can receive up to one thousand dollars from Canadian dividends, savings deposits, term notes, bonds, mortgages, Treasury Bills, and certain capital gains tax-free.

A capital gain is the profit on the disposal of a security or other property. The term "disposal" covers every way you might make a profit, including from: options, futures transactions, and short sales. Only *half* the amount of a capital gain is subject to tax, and must be added to your Gross Income. Tax on capital gains must be paid in the year they are realized, unless the gains can be offset by capital losses.

A capital loss is the opposite of a capital gain. Because capital losses can be used to offset or to reduce capital gains, they are a form of consolation prize. (A point that I make to clients when they take the gas on one of my recommendations.) Capital losses, if you don't have enough offsetting capital gains, can be carried forward indefinitely. But to carry them forward you must *first carry them back* one year. To take advantage of this feature, you have to request an amendment to the previous year's income tax return by filing a prescribed form. Another aspect of excess capital losses is that up to two thousand dollars may be used in any year to reduce Taxable Income from other sources, such as your salary.

To qualify as a capital gain or a capital loss in a given year the disposal must be concluded before the end of that year. This can be tricky, because it is *not* the transaction date (the day the trade was made) but the *settlement date* that counts. In most years, this means that stock and bond trades have to be executed by about the 22nd of December.

Because only half of a capital gain is subject to tax, capital gains provide a much higher return than an equivalent amount of interest or "regular" income. This is especially true for investors in the higher tax brackets. If, for instance, you are in the fifty per cent tax bracket and you make a $10,000 capital gain you only pay $2500 or a twenty-five per cent tax on the total amount.

When computing the cost of a security for capital gains purposes you are allowed to *add* the commission to the purchase. By the same token, to determine the proceeds you are allowed to *deduct* the commission from the sale. Be sure to do this because it *reduces the profit* and *increases the loss* for tax purposes. Here is an example:

Bought 100 shares XYZ Company @ 23.00
+ commission @ .40 = $2340
Cost per share = $23.40
Sold 100 shares XYZ Company @ 30.00
– commission @ .45 = $2955
Proceeds per share = $29.55
Capital gain = $615
50% added to Taxable Income = $307.50

Bank interest and margin interest on loans for investments, as well as investment management fees and safekeeping costs are all deductible from your Gross Income.

Most people think of a capital gain as the clear cut profit on the sale of a stock. But there is another more subtle form of capital gain that can be used to increase the after tax return on a bond. I'm referring to low coupon, deep discount bonds. The yield on bonds with the same maturity varies with the price and the coupon. Let's take two bonds that mature on the same day two years from now. One has a 13% coupon and is priced at 100, the other has a 5% coupon and is priced at 86.44. Both have a gross yield of 13%. However, if you're in the 50% tax bracket, the *after tax* yield on the high coupon bond is 6.5% but it is 8.5% on the low coupon bond. The reason for the after tax difference is that the yield on the discount bond is made up of the 5% coupon—which is fully taxable—and the discount of $13.56 which is capital gain. Investors, particularly those in the high tax brackets, should always consider the after tax yield on a fixed income security—including Guaranteed Investment Certificates.

Before leaving the subject of discount bonds, I should mention that the discount is not always considered as capital gain (the difference between the price you paid and its face value at maturity). If a bond matures in less than twelve months, the discount will likely be treated by National Revenue as income. Also, because Treasury Bills do not pay interest, the discount on Treasury Bills *must* be reported as income. The same treatment applies to Zero Coupon bonds, although no actual interest is received, the theoretical amount of accrued interest should be reported every three years.

Now that we've reviewed the effects of interest income, dividend tax credits, and capitals gains on your Basic Federal Tax, it's time to consider "tax shelters." This is really a misleading term, because most "shelters" merely *defer* tax to a future date.

The most popular tax shelter is the Registered Retirement Savings Plan. The purpose of an RRSP is to build an investment nest egg for your retirement. Contributions to a Registered Retirement Savings Plan can be deducted from your Gross Income. Both the income and capital gains from investments within an RRSP are exempt from tax. You are allowed to have more than one RRSP, and you may transfer funds from one RRSP to another without paying tax.

There is a strict limit on the amount you may contribute each year to RRSP investments. If you don't have a pension plan (or a deferred profit sharing plan) you may contribute twenty per cent of your income to a maximum of $5500 in any one year. If you are already a member of a plan, and contribute less than $3500, you may contribute twenty per cent of your income to a maximum of $3500 per year to an RRSP. Legislation has been tabled in Parliament to raise these limits substantially in 1985 and thereafter. The deadline for RRSP contributions is the end of February or sixty days after the end of the taxation year.

Under present rules you *must* collapse your RRSP when you reach the age of seventy-one (but you may do so at any time before you reach that age). When you collapse your plan you can roll the proceeds directly into an annuity without attracting tax, except on the annual income generated by the annuity. You may also roll the proceeds into a Registered Retirement Income Fund (RRIF) which will pay you a percentage of the total amount on a sliding scale. (A RRIF is *not* the same as a standard annuity, and should only be considered on the basis of professional advice.) Should you simply cash in your plan, the total proceeds will be added to your Gross Income and be taxed in the same year.

A wide range of securities qualify as investments for an RRSP. One of the basic rules to remember is that you can't have more than ten per cent of an RRSP portfolio in foreign securities. (This means that if you do well on a foreign investment and it rises in price to represent more than ten per cent of the portfolio, you must sell some of it.) Among the Canadian investments that qualify are daily interest accounts, term deposits, mortgages, bonds, listed stocks, mutual funds, and insurance plans. Unlisted stocks, commodities and bullion are among the investments that are excluded.

Registered Retirement Savings Plans are offered on a "package" basis by banks, trust companies, brokers, and other financial institutions as well as by some mutual funds and some insurance companies. This type of plan is simple to open—you fill out the forms, plunk down your money, and that's it. Usually, you end up with a term note or shares in a mutual fund. However, the *types of investment* and the *fees* vary widely within this managed spectrum. Therefore, it is prudent to shop around before making a decision. You can also open plans with most brokers and some trust companies which allow *you* to manage your own investments within the RRSP. These are known as self-directed plans. The cost of a self-directed plan is relatively low, and you can control your own financial destiny. However, if you are not an experienced investor, you would be better off to have your plan managed professionally by a fund or an institution.

If you have a self-directed plan you can make contributions in the form of eligible securities rather than cash. For example, you could contribute $3500 worth of Canada Savings Bonds, or one hundred shares of common stock. However, when you transfer securities into your RRSP you can't claim capital losses, *but you must report capital gains*. The only way for you to trigger a capital loss would be to sell the security on the open market and then buy it for your RRSP. Your broker can arrange this type of transaction, which is known as a "cross," and you will have to pay two commissions—one for selling and one for buying. If the capital loss is sufficiently large, it could be worth the extra cost.

Because there is no tax on RRSP investments you can ignore tax credits and after tax returns, and concentrate on *gross* yields. (Also, interest on money borrowed for an RRSP is *not* deductible, nor can you claim the dividend tax credit on RRSP investments.) High yielding investments in an RRSP can compound over a period of years at an astonishing rate. For this reason it makes sense to have a good proportion of the portfolio in fixed income securities. If you have a self-directed plan, you should stagger your debt maturities so that you don't get "locked in." (The hazard of being locked-in is that interest rates will soar and you will not only miss the bonanza, but possibly suffer a decline in the value of your holdings.) One way to get high yields, and to avoid being locked-in, is to buy a variety of maturities. For example, you could buy a series of Zero Coupon bonds. If you did this, you would have both safety and yield, and could count on funds coming due for reinvestment over a set period of time.

Recently, there has been great excitement over the fact that you can now put your home mortgage into your RRSP. Aside from the comfort of paying interest to yourself, it is a questionable advantage. For one thing you will probably have to liquidate a better investment of fund your mortgage. For another, you won't get a special "deal"—the rate must be competitive, you'll have to pay for the mortgage to be insured, and then pay for all the standard costs, including an evaluation of the property.

Unless you plan to retire within the next five years, you should consider holding some equities in your RRSP. The younger you are, the more risk you can take—and over the long term equities have provided a higher rate of return than fixed income securities. In this connection, keep an eye out for good *convertible bonds*, but only select those of companies whose shares you want to own, and don't pay a premium of more than ten per cent for *any* convertible bond. For those with small portfolios (under $10,000) the best way to get an equity exposure is to buy a good mutual fund. For *experienced investors* with *larger portfolios*, you can buy listed stocks for your plan the same way you would outside an RRSP.

Regardless of your experience, and the amount of your holdings, *act your age*. When you're young you can afford to invest in high risk/high reward situations such as high tech stocks, but if you're going to retire within the next few years, *all* your portfolio should be in short term fixed income investments.

If you're in the twenty per cent tax bracket or higher, you should have an RRSP. It is an excellent tax shelter because your contributions reduce your Taxable Income, and your investments are free from tax. Of course, the big pay-off (we hope) comes from an RRSP when you retire and convert it into a fat annuity. As I mentioned earlier, you must pay tax on the *income* generated by the annuity.

For those of you who would like detailed information on Registered Retirement Savings Plans, I would recommend two books. One is *RRSP Strategies*, by David Louis, which is published by Hume Publishing Company, Willowdale, Ontario (The same people that publish *The Money Letter*). The other book is titled *1984 No-Nonsense Guide to RRSPs and RHOSPs and other Tax Shelters*, by Steven Kelman, which is published by the *Financial Times of Canada*.

Planning for your retirement is all very well, but for most young people it is a remote eventuality. Their first priority is to buy a home. This brings us to another type of tax shelter, the Registered Home Ownership Savings Plan or RHOSP.

A RHOSP allows you to contribute $1000 a year to a maximum of $10,000 towards the purchase of a home. The amount you contribute is deductible from your Taxable Income. (Residents of Quebec, however, can't claim this deduction against their provincial income.) Like an RRSP, you have to sign some forms to open a RHOSP and an institution must be the custodian of the funds. When you collapse your RHOSP—providing you buy a home within sixty days—the proceeds are tax-free. The definition of a "home" includes most types of dwellings including a cottage, a trailer, or a houseboat. (Don't underestimate a houseboat, I've seen some in Vancouver that are nicer than most regular houses.)

To qualify for a RHOSP you must be eighteen years of age and a Canadian resident. If you or your spouse have not had a RHOSP or do not own a home or cottage, you can *both* open RHOSPs. In this case, you can each contribute $1000 a year for total of $2000 and a maximum of $20,000. However, if you own a cottage or a MURB (MURBs will be discussed later) or have collapsed a RHOSP, you are excluded from the plan. In the case of a person who collapses a RHOSP and doesn't buy a home, the proceeds from the RHOSP are added to Gross Income and are taxable in that year.

The most suitable investments for a RHOSP are high yielding fixed income securities. You might also include some shares in one of the more conservative mutual funds. Because of the relatively short term (assuming you can contribute $1000 for ten consecutive years) there's no obvious advantage to equities—and no justification to speculate. The deadline for contributing to a RHOSP is the thirty first of December.

One of the latest tax wrinkles is the ISIP or Indexed Security Investment Plan. The purpose of an ISIP is to reduce capital gains on your investments by the amount of the inflation rate. It is fairly complicated and might be best explained if I use an example. Suppose you have five hundred shares of stock in an ISIP that cost you $30 per share. During the year you sell them for $35 per share for a capital gain of $5 per share. However, if inflation was running at twelve per cent the cost of the shares (for tax purposes) would be increased by twelve per cent or $3.60 per share. Therefore the cost would be $33.60 and the capital gain would be reduced to $1.40 per share. This is the good news.

The bad news is that you must pay tax each year on capital gains within an ISIP *even though you have not sold* the securities. The tax applies to twenty five per cent of the capital gain, and the balance of capital gain is carried forward to the next year.

You can open an ISIP with your broker, who will charge you a fee of around one hundred dollars to manage the plan. Among other things, your broker must compute the cost base of your ISIP holdings each month after taking into account the inflation factor. One half of the fees for your ISIP may be deducted from your Gross Income, but you can't deduct interest charged on money borrowed for ISIP investments. Also, dividends and capital gains in an ISIP don't qualify for the $1000 Investment Income Deduction. Until the end of 1984, you can sell your losers to your ISIP and claim a capital loss on the sales—even though you still own the securities. This little loophole will be closed on 1 January 1985.

There are pros and cons to an ISIP, so before making a move in this direction you should have a chat with your accountant. Basically it boils down to this: during periods of low inflation an ISIP holds little appeal, but if inflation heats up—as it inevitably will—an ISIP will be a useful tax shelter.

The province of Quebec has a tax shelter called the Quebec Stock Savings Plan. Residents of the province may contribute up to twenty per cent of their income, to a maximum of $20,000 (less RRSP and pension contributions) each year. Contributions are deductible from provincial Taxable Income in varying amounts, depending upon what type of securities are purchased.

Only new issues of shares are eligible for the plan. New issues that qualify include common shares with voting rights and convertible preferred shares of listed companies that are based in Quebec, or of companies that have more than 50% of their operations in Quebec. To stimulate investment in developing companies, residents can deduct 150% of the cost of buying shares of Quebec companies with assets of less than 25 million. The deduction for shares in companies with more than 1 billion in assets is 75% and this will be reduced to 50% in 1985.

To be completely tax-free, the sum invested in the QSSP must be maintained at the same level for two years following the year the shares were purchased. During this period the original shares can be sold *providing* they are replaced to the same value by other eligible shares. Capital gains and capital losses resulting from the disposal of eligible shares in a QSSP are treated for tax purposes the same as gains and losses outside the plan. Also, dividends on shares within the plan qualify for the Canadian dividend tax credit.

As with any tax shelter, Quebec residents should look first at the quality of the investment before grabbing the tax deduction. I know of some pretty scruffy new issues that have been sold in Quebec simply on the basis of the tax deduction. If you are a Quebec resident don't make this mistake. The Quebec Stock Savings Plan is a good deal, but this doesn't mean that you can invest blindly—you have to use sound judgement.

This warning also applies to Ontario residents who buy shares of Small Business Development Corporations. An SBDC is a holding company that invests venture capital in Ontario businesses engaged in certain fields such as tourism, publishing, and research. The incentive here is that the Ontario government reimburses new issue buyers up to thirty per cent of the cost of their purchase. This still leaves seventy per cent of your money at risk. I'm all for helping small business and promoting investment in that area, but I would strongly suggest that you look before you leap.

It's hard to overemphasize the folly of buying a tax shelter for its deduction rather than its merit as an investment. If it's a poor investment, you'd be a hell of a lot better to give the money to charity. You'd get a full write-off, and at least you'd feel good about it. Doctors and dentists—who have high incomes and are busy people—are particularly prone to losing their money in tax shelters.

Recent legislation has pretty well eliminated the major benefits of investing in Multiple Unit Residential Buildings or MURBS. This real estate tax shelter was originally designed to encourage private investment in rental housing. Today, if you own a MURB you can still reduce your Taxable Income through Capital Cost Allowances and a few other deductions. (Except for MURBs, you can't deduct real estate losses caused by Capital Cost Allowances from other income.)

The way a MURB works is that you invest a small amount to purchase one or more units in a new apartment building or multiple unit dwelling. The balance of your purchase price is financed by a mortgage. If all goes well, you get your tax write-offs, and later sell the property for a profit—which will probably be taxed as a capital gain.

Many MURBs have been poor investments because the real estate promoter has inflated the purchase price of the property far above its true market value. This meant that investors paid too much for their units and started out behind the eight ball. Also, in some cases the potential occupancy rate has been over-stated and rental income from the project has failed to cover the mortgage costs. When this happens, you as an investor must reach into your pocket and pay the mortgage. If the situation deteriorates sufficiently, the mortgage company can foreclose. You are on the hook for the mortgage—and you could be in serious financial trouble. I have a number of successful real estate people as clients, but none of them invest in MURBs. This tells me something.

The same tax principles and the same hazards apply to hotels and vessels as tax shelters. Here again, the write-offs are not worth the candle if it's a poor investment.

Canadian films have the dubious honour of being the worst tax shelter. I'm not sure whether it's the element of glamour or the generous write-offs that prompt people to invest in Canadian films. It certainly can't be the profits, because hardly any of the movies make money—even it they're a success at the box office—and the accounting is so loose that budget figures are often a joke. I am sympathetic to the Canadian movie industry, and would like to see it flourish. But I think that if you're going to throw your money away, there are more enjoyable ways to do it. For this reason I have never bought a film for myself nor have I ever sold one to a client. (However, my brother-in-law dropped about $300,000 investing in Canadian films.) My advice to you is that if you want to get involved in movies, buy a video recorder.

Canadian oil and gas drilling funds are a high risk but sometimes profitable tax shelter. This was especially true during the early days of exploration in the Beaufort Sea. (Some of those drilling funds allowed deductions of as much as 166% of the total cost.) Nowadays, when you buy a drilling fund you can only write-off 100% of the amount of your investment that is actually expended on exploration. You can also qualify for other exemptions, such as 10% of the property expenses and 30% of the development expenses. In some cases you can be credited with a PIP grant (Petroleum Incentive Payment). If the drilling program is successful, you will receive a share of the revenues from the sale of oil or gas.

The operator or manager of the drilling fund is the General Partner, and the outside investors are Limited Partners. Every deal is different, but a typical arrangement is for the Limited Partners to receive 80% of the profits and the General Partner 20% of the profits until the original investment has been recovered. After this happens, it is quite common for a fifty-fifty split in the profits. Often, the General Partner will subsequently make the Limited Partners a cash offer or a share offer for their interest in the drilling fund.

There are several hazards you must face when you invest in a drilling fund. The most obvious is that the exploration program will come up with dry holes. Or the operator will find gas rather than oil, in which case the gas wells will probably be capped. Or the success will be so modest that it will take years to recover your investment. In the meantime—and this is true of most tax shelters—you hold an investment that is very difficult to sell to someone else.

If you're going to invest in a drilling fund, the first thing you must do is to carefully read the prospectus. The most important factor is the integrity of the General Partner. Once this has been established, find out what the past record has been. Has the General Partner been successful, not only in making discoveries, but in making a *profit* for the Limited Partners? What is the risk factor—is it a deep drilling program in "elephant country," or is it a series of low risk (and usually low return) shallow wells? Will the drilling program take place in familiar territory, or will it be a pure exploration play? If the exploration is primarily for gas, are there contracts in hand that can be used to sell the gas? These are some of the answers you need before you make your investment decision.

The most recent innovation in tax shelters are Research and Development units. The federal government introduced this concept to help companies—particularly those in the high tech industry—to get money for the outlay they had made on research. Canadian companies can claim research and development costs as an expense, but in many cases the companies don't have sufficient income to take advantage of this deduction. By allowing the companies to sell their tax credits to individual investors the government encourages further research and development. For the investor, an R & D Fund can be a relatively low risk tax shelter.

There are two basic ways an R & D shelter is structured. One type involves the purchase by the investor of an Equity unit in the company at an inflated price. A large portion of the price, however, is tax deductible. For instance, Mitel sold an R & D unit for $42.50 which consisted of one $25 par convertible preferred share and a tax deduction of thirty-four per cent from Basic Federal Tax. For residents of Ontario, the thirty-four per cent deduction from Basic Federal Tax reduced provincial tax so that the total deduction amounted to 50.73% of the value of the unit. Because the tax deduction amounted to $21.56 (50.73% of $42.50) the effective cost of the $25 par preferred share was $20.94— which made it attractive. Mitel raised about $90 million on this offering.

The other form of R & D shelter is called an "Instant Retractable" or more commonly a "flip." No equity is involved in this type of transaction, but the investor receives an immediate refund of fifty per cent of the purchase price, and is paid a bonus for buying the R & D unit. The incentive to the investor is the bonus, which may range from one per cent to more than ten per cent of the value of the unit. (If there was no bonus an investor wouldn't buy a "flip" because he would simply be making an advance payment on his income tax.) The federal tax deduction on a flip is the same as for an equity deal, e.g., thirty-four per cent of the value of the purchase. As a result of the federal deduction, there is also a reduction in provincial tax. Supposing that in 1983 an Ontario investor bought a "flip" with a six per cent bonus. (I had a number of clients who actually did this.) Here's how it worked: The investor gave the company a cheque for $100,000 and got in return a cheque from the company for $56,000 ($50,000 + 6% of $100,000 = $56,000) plus a $34,000 credit on his Basic Federal Tax. The "flow-through" of the thirty-four per cent credit reduced his provincial tax so that his total deduction amounted to 50.73%—the same as an R & D equity unit.

From an investment point of view the two types of R & D tax shelters are fundamentally different. If you are going to buy an Equity unit, you must *assess the quality of the underlying stock*, because it may decline in value. (By the same token, you have an opportunity for capital gain, because the shares may increase in value.) An Instant Retractable R & D unit offers no potential for gain, except for the bonus. On the other hand, providing the documentation is *properly* done, and your cheque is held *in trust* until a formal *ruling* is received from the Department of National Revenue, there is virtually no risk in an R & D "flip."

My only qualification—and it's an important one—would be to have *any* R & D deal checked out by an experienced lawyer and an accountant before you sign on the dotted line.

I have purposely left the best tax shelter of all to the end—your home. Assuming that it is your principal residence (and you can only have *one* principal residence at a time) when you sell your home the proceeds are tax-free. In the interim, you have the use and enjoyment of it. You can't beat that.

CHAPTER 15

Forecasting Prices

THE WEATHER CAN be predicted with far greater certainty than stock market prices. This, despite the fact that millions of man hours and computer hours have been spent trying to forecast the future price of stocks. The reason forecasting can't be reduced to a science is because the market is profoundly influenced by human emotions. You can't program emotions—such as greed and fear—into a computer. This is a comfort, for if we knew exactly what was going to happen it would take the fun out of the game.

Some market *savants* have been able to forecast prices with incredible accuracy for brief periods of time while others have made brilliant but isolated calls. So far, no one has been right all the time. This shouldn't discourage you from trying to predict market moves, but it should tell you that forecasting is a formidable challenge.

Forecasting prices applies to both buying and selling decisions. It encompasses not only *what* to buy, but *when* to buy it, and when to *sell* it. Recently, an old friend complained to me that brokers were great at telling clients when to buy stocks but they never seemed to tell clients when to sell them. This was true to some extent in the past, but I think today most analysts will as joyfully jump on a sell recommendation as they will a buy recommendation.

Investors and those who intend to invest should know the

rudiments of market forecasting, if only to understand the diagrams and reports that are published by research analysts. To this end I will try to briefly outline the main methods used to predict price movements. This chapter may also help to lift the veil of mystery that surrounds the technical side of the investment business. Who knows, you may decide to try your own hand at forecasting. If you're right more often than you're wrong, you'll make money.

The first thing an analyst must do is to assess the stage of the economic cycle. This is crucial to any investment decision because *the market leads the economy* by six months to a year—sometimes longer. In other words, stock prices today reflect anticipated developments far down the road. What this means is that you must look into the future to establish today's values. You can't simply base your assumptions on the present. If you fail to look ahead you can have a nasty surprise or miss a golden opportunity. To illustrate the importance of the business cycle, and the way the market anticipates the future, let's track the price of Alcan shares from 1980 to 1983. Alcan's earnings are expressed in U.S. dollars and this period covers the worst recession since the Great Depression:

1980—Economy in final stage of upswing, business booming, Alcan earned $6.70 per share. Stock hit high of $52⅝

1981—Economy tops out and starts into decline, Alcan earned $3.24 per share. Stock hit high of $55 and low of $36⅞

1982—Economy in doldrums, Alcan *lost* $.69 per share. After hitting low of $24⅞ stock recovered to $42.

1983—Economy starts to recover, but Alcan lost in the first quarter and only made $1.20 for the year. Yet stock rose to $53⅝, which was higher than when the company earned $6.70 in 1980.

There are several interesting things to note in this example. Alcan's price declined to $36⅞ in 1981 when it earned $3.24 per share, but the following year (when the company had *no earnings* and actually lost money) far-sighted investors saw the coming recovery and bid the shares up to $42. In 1983, when the recovery was confirmed, Alcan stock hit $53⅝ even though earnings were less than one fifth of what they had been in 1980. Alcan's roller coaster ride was entirely due to the economic cycle, and at every stage its share price reflected *anticipated* rather than actual earnings.

Investment forecasters study all sorts of political and economic cycles. Here are five of the better known cycles with their normal durations:

Kitchin Cycle	4 years
Juglar Cycle	8-11 years
Wardwell Cycle	11-16 years
Kuznet Cycle	22 years
Kondratieff Cycle	54 years

There is no need for the average investor to get involved in the study of cycles, except to establish where one is in the current business cycle. However, as a point of interest, the Kondratieff Cycle or Kondratieff Wave correctly pinpointed the Great Depression. It was devised by Nikolai Kondratieff, a Russian economist, who was dispatched to a Siberian labour camp in 1930 for his political views. According to the Kondratieff Cycle, North America will be in a terminal economic phase by the end of this century. (Some goldbugs believe that we're *already* in big trouble.)

When mentioning cycles I should add that many people believe that hemlines reflect the state of the economy, ie., in the Twenties both stock prices and hemlines were high, but during the Depression hemlines came down with the market. Today, a favourite theory is that the winner of the Super Bowl will determine the direction of the market in the coming year. If one of the original NFL teams wins, it will be an "up" year for the market, but if one of the former AFL teams wins, it will be a "down" year. You can take these theories with a handful of salt.

In addition to studying cycles, forecasters and economists use other methods to foretell the future. All of these methods are based on assumptions which make them highly susceptible to human error.

A favourite method is to employ the "Old Grey Mare" theory by comparing the present situation with a past period and then projecting a similar outcome. The flaw with this theory is that although history repeats itself, forecasters are inclined to jump to a conclusion first, and then try to justify it by comparing apples with oranges. On the fiftieth anniversary of the 1929 stock market crash many pundits wrote scare articles using the "Old Grey Mare" theory to liken the situation in 1979 to 1929. Because the two periods were not comparable, these articles were rubbish.

One of the most pleasant ways to predict the economy is by "Consensus Forecasting." In this method like-minded analysts confer with each other and reach a joint conclusion. If it's wrong, nobody blames the other fellow, because everyone's in the same boat.

Then we have "Ivory Tower" or "Econometric Model" forecasting which is complex and fraught with all manner of perils. In this method an immense amount of data is fed through computers to project a theoretical state of the economy at some future date. The Bank of Canada and the Conference Board of Canada use econometric models. The problems with this type of exercise are staggering, and may be summed up with the phrase "garbage in, garbage out."

Among the data fed to computers to make an econometric model are a number of economic indicators. These indicators—by themselves—can provide valuable information. They include such things as the number of housing starts, new car sales, unemployment, the amount of excess plant capacity, the rate of inflation, the measure of consumer confidence, and other significant figures. If you watch these indicators (which are published in the press and available from some of the better brokerage firms), you will be on surer ground, and can judge for yourself where the economy is heading.

The money supply and the prevailing interest rate are two key indicators to note. The money supply determines the *availability* of money while the interest rate establishes the *cost* of money. To get a handle on the money supply look at the figure "M-I" (which refers to total currency in circulation and demand deposits). This figure is published in the financial papers and is also available from your broker. The interest rate, as mentioned in the chapter on bonds, is established each week by the Treasury Bill auction. Money becomes more expensive as the interest rate rises, and cheaper as the rate falls. Money becomes easier to borrow as the supply increases but "tighter" as the money supply decreases. If the money supply increases while the interest rate is rising, money is not "tight" but merely expensive. The worst scenario for business is a rising interest rate *and* a decreasing money supply. The best is a declining interest rate with an expanding money supply.

Because money is the lifeblood of the economy, interest rates have a tremendous effect upon the financial markets. During an expansionary phase, inflation forces rates higher due to competition by the private sector and government for funds. At some point in the inflationary cycle the government usually steps in to check inflation by manipulating rates even higher. This stops the inflationary spiral by inducing an economic recession. It is a harsh measure, akin to burning a fire break to stop a forest fire. Opposite is a diagram showing how rising interest rates have precipitated every recession for the past thirty years.

This diagram reveals how sensitive the economy is to interest rates. It also shows how rates are trending higher, because the peaks and valleys are rising—a rate of 5½% triggered a recession in 1958 but it took more than twice that rate to set off a recession in 1974, and rates in excess of 16% to cause a recession five years later. This suggests that the economy has gradually managed to accommodate higher rates of interest. The danger signal to watch for is an inverted yield curve—when short rates exceed long term rates. *This invariably spells disaster for the financial markets.*

Before leaving the subject of money and interest rates you should bear in mind that:

1. Money is always invested (unless it's in transit.)
2. All the financial markets are interconnected.
3. Money inevitably flows to the highest rate of return with the lowest perceived risk.

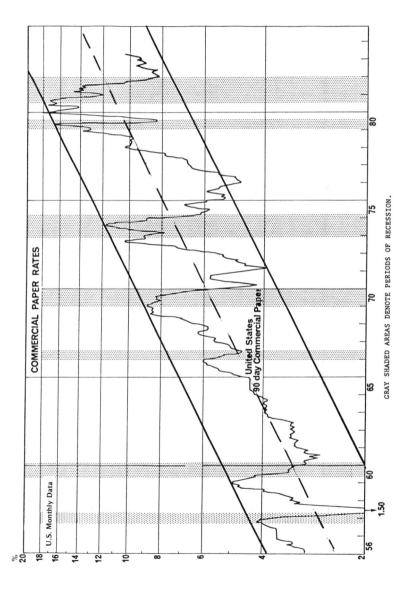

COMMERCIAL PAPER RATES

U.S. Monthly Data

United States
90 day Commercial Paper

GRAY SHADED AREAS DENOTE PERIODS OF RECESSION.

The first two points are straightforward, but the last point deserves some explanation. If stock yields dwindle and bond rates rise, at some stage money will leave the stock market and be reinvested in fixed income securities. As a result, the stock market will take the gas. Conversely, if bonds yields decline precipitously, money will be shifted from the bond market into the stock market. This influx of funds will fuel a surge in stock prices.

Having looked at the background of the financial markets, we'll move on to the task of predicting prices for individual stocks. There are literally hundreds of ways or "systems" that are used to forecast stock prices, which range from astrology to reading computer print-outs. For simplicity, we can divide analysts into two camps: fundamentalists and technicians.

A fundamentalist takes a long term view and uses a quantitive approach. This means that he assesses the shares of a company in relation to others in the industry, pores over the balance sheet of the company, examines the quality of its management, and measures its products against the competition. He is also concerned with the past record of earnings, dividend yields, plant capacity and business in general. In short, a fundamentalist turns over every rock in sight. After making an in-depth study of the company, he then arrives at his decision whether its shares should be bought or sold.

Don Tigert is the senior merchandising analyst in our firm. He spends a lot of time interviewing senior management and working out financial ratios, but he also gets down to the grass roots level. In fact, Don is so involved in the merchandising field that even when he is travelling on his holidays he can't resist checking out stores and supermarkets. To keep abreast of industry developments, Don has a network of store managers across the country who phone him when their company comes up with a new marketing wrinkle. As a result, he is exceptionally well informed, and his opinion on merchandising stocks is highly valued by financial institutions and other major investors. Don is the best example I know of a fundamentalist.

Speaking of fundamental analysis reminds me of Olivia, who was one of my first clients. She was a delightfully eccentric woman who somehow managed, through the quirkiest form of logic, to pick winning stocks. One day she phoned and gave me an order to buy one thousand shares of Dupont. I was a little surprised, because Dupont's earnings were declining, and I asked her why she liked the stock. Olivia replied that she was bullish on Dupont because of the hula hoop craze, and she expected the company to sell zillions of tons of plastic for hula hoops. As it turned out, Dupont didn't cash in on the hula hoop boom, but Olivia made money because the stock went up for other reasons.

A technician usually takes a short term view and employs an entirely different approach. He couldn't care less about dividend yields, Price/Earnings ratios, or the nuts and bolts of a company. A technician believes that all this information is distilled into the current price of the stock. He studies such things as advance/decline ratios, short interest numbers, odd-lot figures, and moving averages to project future prices. His main tool in this exercise is a chart of the stock on graph paper which shows its recent price pattern. So important is a chart to a technician, that with a chart in hand he doesn't even need to know the name of a company to pass judgement on it.

It's easy to criticize technical analysis (one definition of a technician is a fundamentalist who has lost money) but you can't afford to ignore it. For one thing, a great many investors follow charts and believe in them. This means that when certain price movements occur a lot of investors react in the same way. These investors may be misguided, but stock prices change as a result of their mass buying or selling. As an analogy, suppose everyone believed that if seven seagulls flew over the Statue of Liberty at the stroke of noon on a Tuesday, the Dow Jones Industrial Average would go up one hundred points. This might be absurd, but if enough people believed it and seven seagulls floated over the statue at high noon on a Tuesday, the Dow would take off like a cut cat. The other reason you can't ignore technical analysis is that quite often, it works.

The granddaddy of technical analysis was Charles H. Dow, who from 1889 to 1902 was editor of *The Wall Street Journal*. It was he who developed the averages on the New York Stock Exchange that bear his name. The most famous of these averages is the Dow Jones Industrial Average, which is comprised of thirty widely held NYSE stocks. When a client rings a broker to ask what the market is doing, and is told the market is "up three points" the broker is referring to the Dow Jones Industrial Average on the New York Stock Exchange, or "Big Board." As an aside, there's only one "big board" and that's in New York—if a client asks what the Canadian market is doing, he is given the Toronto Stock Exchange Composite Index which is comprised of three hundred stocks.

Charles Dow developed the Dow Theory, which projects market trends based on the correlation in price movements of the Dow Jones Industrial Average, the Transportation Average and the Utility Average. In recent years, because rail stocks only represent about three per cent of the value of listed New York stocks, the Transportation Average has lost importance, and the significance of the utilities, due to their nuclear problems, has also been questioned. In addition, the thirty stocks that comprise the Industrial Average are considered a poor barometer of the stock market because they're all "blue chips" and they are so few in number. As a result, the Dow Theory has come to be regarded as suspect by many people. (Both the Standard & Poor's Index, which is based on five hundred stocks, and the Valueline Index are regarded as much truer reflections of the market's overall behaviour.) Nevertheless, a lot of investors still follow the Dow Theory, and the Dow Jones Industrial Index moves in a surprisingly similar manner to the broader based averages.

In the mid-Thirties another American, Ralph N. Elliot, developed a market theory known as the Elliot Wave Principle. This is a complex theory that is difficult to master, and once mastered it requires sound judgement to interpret. It might be described as a refinement, with variations, of the Dow Theory. Some analysts have had excellent success using the Elliot Wave Principle.

Even if you have no interest in technical analysis, you might like to keep an eye on a few of the more widely followed technical indicators. With this in mind, I will mention some of the more popular ones, and explain their use.

The simplest is "Volume" which is the number of shares traded in a particular stock or the whole market on a given day. An upward move without a corresponding increase in volume is considered a weak signal, while an upward move on heavy volume is very bullish. A downward move on low volume is a bad sign (indicating an absence of buyers) and a downward move on heavy volume is *very* bearish.

Insider Trading Reports (which are published in the press) reveal what the informed players are doing. Due to their senior positions, insiders have a very good batting average regardless of whether they are buying or selling. Insider reports can provide a tip-off, but they can also be misleading in the case of sales because you don't know *why* the insider sold. The company might be in trouble, but then again, the insider may simply have needed money.

The ten Most Active stocks on the major exchanges are listed each day on the financial pages (and usually mentioned in the market reports). These show where the action is, and can indicate a potential opportunity. It is important to watch the most active list if you hold stocks. If one of yours is among the top ten traders, you should find out why.

On the same page as the Most Active stocks you will see two columns: one is headed "New Highs" the other "New Lows." If you've been thinking of buying a stock and it appears in the New Lows column it might be time to buy—*after* you have checked on the company's current position. If you hold a stock that appears in the New Highs, you might review your position. (I didn't say sell it, I said review your position.)

The size of Option Premiums, and the Ratio of Puts to Calls are two sentiment indicators. The average size of option premiums reveals how much enthusiasm is behind the market. The ratio of Puts to Calls indicates whether the public is bullish or bearish—normally, call options are much more popular than put options, because people would rather bet on stocks going up than down.

The Short Interest Ratio is an interesting tool because it indicates how many shares have been sold short. Normally, the *higher* the short interest the more bullish it is for the market. The reason for this is that all those shares that have been shorted will eventually have to be bought back—which of course means that there is a buying reserve in the wings. Also, if the market suddenly turns up, and there's a heavy short position, it can cause a buying panic.

The Odd Lot indices show what the little investor, the person who can't afford to buy board lots, is doing. If the odd lotters are heavy buyers or heavy sellers, the professionals take the *opposite* stance, on the premise that the little guy is usually wrong. Sad to say, the professionals consistently make money this way.

It is useful to watch the Market Breadth figures which give the number of issues traded, and breakdown the number of advancing and declining stocks. It is not unusual for the market averages to point in one direction and the breadth figures in the opposite direction. Breadth gives you a good idea of the undertone of the whole market.

A growing number of people follow the "contrarian theory." A contrarian believes that the crowd is usually wrong. Contrarians reason that if everyone is recommending a stock, eventually the buying will be exhausted and the stock will be an excellent short. By the same token, if a stock is being dumped by everyone, eventually the selling will dry up and it will be a good buy. People of this bent watch the Barron's Confidence Index, and read publications that poll the opinions of investment advisory services.

Traditionally, General Motors has been regarded as a bellwether stock. How GM goes, so goes the rest of the market. Lately, Merrill Lynch has also been considered a bellwether stock on the premise that if the market goes up, so do the earnings of the Thundering Herd (and vice versa). The price of gold is another barometer, because historically the price of the yellow metal has moved *opposite* to the stock market.

Most technicians keep Moving Averages of the market and moving averages of specific stocks. A moving average is compiled by taking the average price over a period of weeks—the shorter the duration the more sensitive the average. The most common time frames for moving averages are 13, 26, and 52 weeks. A moving average is charted as a line on graph paper, and indicates a change in direction for the stock when the current price goes above or below that line. The inherent danger of moving averages is that they can give false signals. Should the current price cross *back again*, you will be whip-sawed if you bought or sold the stock when it first broke through the line.

Having mentioned time frames I should try and define for you "long term," "intermediate term," and "short term." I say try, because nothing is written in stone. (I have a gunslinger client who considers a stock bought and sold before lunch to be a "short term" trade and one held overnight to be "long term" investment.) Generally speaking, in the investment business "long term" refers to a year or more, "intermediate term" means three months to a year, and "short term" is from one month to three months.

A chart provides the price history of a stock in the form of a jagged line. Technicians study the pattern of the jagged lines and from it project the *probable* future course of the stock. Two assumptions are made when reading charts:

1. Prices move in trends.
2. A change in trend is usually signalled in advance by a characteristic pattern or formation.

Reading a stock chart has been likened to making a medical diagnosis. If you miss one symptom (technical indicator) or misread the pattern you will arrive at the wrong conclusion. An oft heard lament of technicians is that their chart was right, but they misread it. To help you understand what charting is all about, I will explain a few of the basics and some of the jargon used in this form of technical analysis.

First, I should mention that charts are plotted on graph paper and there are two ways of recording price changes. One is by means of a "Point and Figure" chart, the other by means of a "Bar" chart. A Point and Figure chart records the price movements throughout the trading day in proper sequence. From this chronological pattern it is possible to predict short term targets with accuracy. Prices are recorded with noughts and crosses, one symbol being used exclusively for "upticks" the other symbol for "downticks." (You can use whichever symbol you wish, but you must be consistent). The illustration on the following page shows the way a Point and Figure chart is plotted—in this example the noughts represent downticks, the crosses upticks.

A Bar chart, which is much easier to read than a Point and Figure chart, uses a single vertical line to cover the trading range of the stock for the day. The bottom of the line corresponds to the stock's lowest price, the top of the line to the stock's highest price. A horizontal line marks the price at which the stock closed on that day. At the bottom of a Bar chart are vertical lines which indicate the trading volume each day. The second diagram on this page shows a section of a Bar chart.

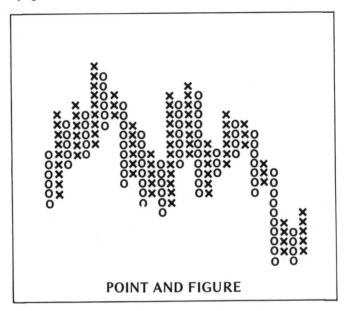

POINT AND FIGURE

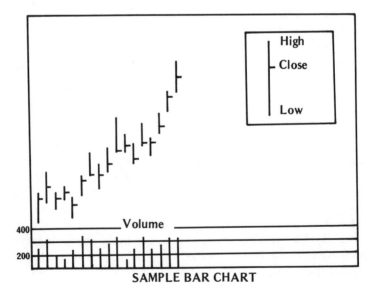

SAMPLE BAR CHART

Earlier, I mentioned that one of the basic assumptions in charting is that stocks move in trends. These trends can easily be identified, and usually last for an appreciable length of time. Chartists often highlight trends with parallel lines to mark their channel. Here's a diagram showing both an Uptrend and a Downtrend.

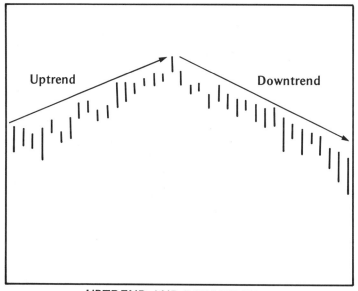

UPTREND AND DOWNTREND

When a stock has no discernible trend, but "backs and fills" forming a flat saw-toothed pattern, it is said to be in a Congestion Area. This is caused by the buying and selling pressures on the stock being roughly in balance. In other words, it's a tug-of-war that's in progress. Eventually, the stock price will break out of the Congestion Area on the upside or the downside. After this happens, the Congestion Area becomes a Resistance Level or a Support Level.

If the stock broke on the downside, the Congestion Area becomes a Resistance Level. This is caused by the fact that many investors who bought in the Congestion Area and then saw the stock decline, will sell their stock "if it ever gets back to what I paid for it." Because of the overhanging supply factor, it will be difficult for the stock to move higher. Hence the term "Resistance Level."

Should the stock chew through the supply and move above the Resistance Level, the Resistance Level will then become a Support Level. The logic behind this is that many of those who sold, and then saw the stock continue to move ahead will be waiting to buy back again if the shares decline to the price at which they sold them. These buyers will act as a barrier to a further decline, and will create a Support Level.

This diagram shows Resistance and Support levels:

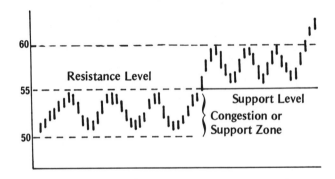

One of the most ominous, and easiest to recognize reversal patterns is the Head and Shoulders formation. This is usually seen after a stock has had a major advance, and indicates that the stock has "topped out" and is about to have a significant decline. It looks exactly like its name.

If you turn the Head and Shoulders picture upside down, you will get an extremely bullish pattern which is known as an Inverse Head and Shoulders or Triple Bottom. This usually occurs at the end of a long sell-off and signals that the stock is about to move up again.

A Double Top is another warning reversal pattern. It has the

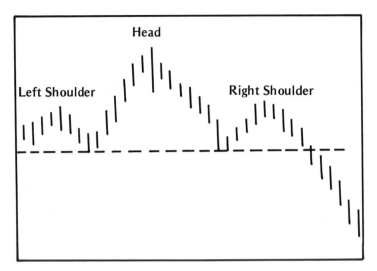

HEAD AND SHOULDERS

same connotation as a Head and Shoulders formation. The opposite of a Double Top is a Double Bottom, which indicates that selling has been exhausted and the line of least resistance for the stock is up. Here is a Double Bottom:

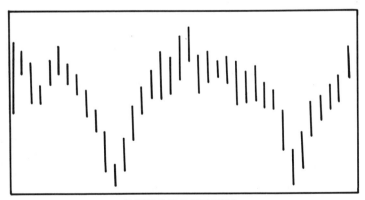

DOUBLE BOTTOM

Triangular formations can also signal a break-out either on the upside or the downside—depending upon whether the horizontal side is on the top or the bottom of the triangle. An Ascending Triangle, which has it's horizontal side on the top, is formed by the stock reaching a similar limit on each upward movement, but successively higher low points. The action looks like a coiled spring. The break-out from an Ascending Triangle is to higher levels. A Descending Triangle is the reverse of an Ascending Triangle, and signals a downward movement. This is what an Ascending Triangle looks like:

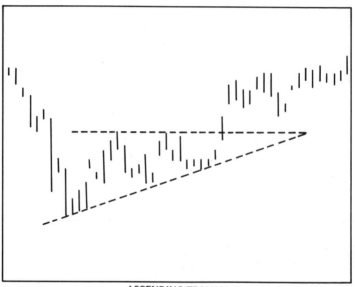

ASCENDING TRIANGLE

Flags are dynamic small formations that indicate a continuation of a trend. They consist of a "pole" and a "flag." The "pole" is a sharp upward or downward movement, and the "flag" which follows is a minor trend in the *opposite* direction. The break-out in the original direction usually approximates the length of the "pole." The theory behind this pattern is that the minor fluctuations in the "flag" imply that reactionary buying or selling is contained and that the original trend will reassert itself. Here is an Upward Flag:

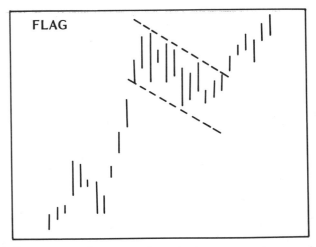

A Gap occurs when a stock trades in a range above or below the previous day's range and leaves a clear space in the chart. This is a strong signal that can happen on an upside or a downside move. It is usually caused by overnight news that precipitates a wave of buying or selling. As long as the Gap is not filled in, the trend will continue. However, if the stock retraces its path and trades in the level of the Gap, this means that the news that caused the Gap has now been fully discounted. Here is an illustration that shows two gaps:

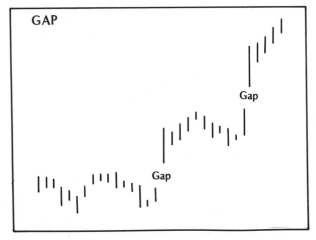

And now, for review purposes, here's a larger section of a chart that shows several of the patterns I have mentioned.

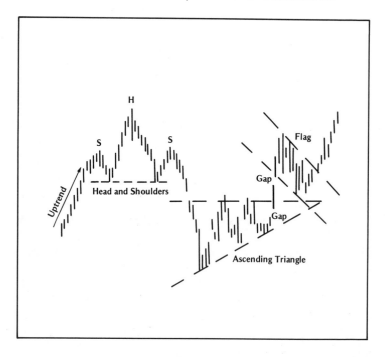

What I like about technical indicators and the study of charts is that they can identify short term trading opportunities and they can also flash a warning signal. However, I would not rely *solely* upon technical analysis to make investment decisions. This is a personal opinion, but it is one that is shared by most successful investors.

The main drawback with technical analysis is that it is based on the law of probability—which means that even the most astute technician can be mislead. This is also true of fundamental analysis, but a good fundamentalist will make less dramatic errors, and there is usually more time to correct a bad recommendation.

For this reason, I place the greatest emphasis on the fundamental approach. When I'm looking at an investment situation I first study the fundamentals, and then check the technical picture. If the technical picture and the fundamentals disagree, I go back to the drawing board. But when the two approaches indicate the same conclusion, I move ahead with confidence.

If you want to learn more about fundamental analysis, I would suggest that you read *Security Analysis*, by Graham and Dodd, which is published by McGraw Hill. This book was written decades ago, and is still the definitive work on the subject.

Should you wish to delve deeper into the technical side of the game I would recommend the book *Technical Analysis of Stock Trends*, by Edwards and Magee, which is published by John Magee Inc. For those who are interested in charts, you can subscribe to a Canadian service which will send you updated stock charts each month. It is called the "Graphoscope®" and is available from GPS Publishing Limited, Toronto.

To close this chapter I would like to tell you about the most memorable market forecast that was ever given to me. It was in 1958, when I was a sales trainee with Royal Securities at their head office on St. James Street in Montreal. At that time the senior executives of the firm were on the fifth floor of the building, while the sales staff occupied the ground floor. One day I got into the elevator to go to the fifth floor on an errand. I was joined by a very old and immensely rich senior partner who was reputed to have made millions in the market. Being the youngest and most junior salesman in the firm, I was in awe of my companion. The ancient elevator, which was lit by a single electric bulb, creaked slowly upward as the two of us stood together in silence.

Although I felt nervous, it occurred to me that this was a great opportunity to cadge a pearl of wisdom. Screwing up my courage, I said:

"Sir, what do you think the market's going to do?"

The old gentleman heard the question, but did not answer. Finally, when we reached the top floor, he turned and slowly waved a mottled hand up and down in front of me. As he made this motion he said in a dusty whisper:

"Young man, the market will continue to fluctuate."

CHAPTER 16

Strategies & Pitfalls

THE MOST OBVIOUS investment strategy is to buy low and to sell high. This is easier said than done, but there are certain ways that you can avoid the pitfalls and increase your profits in the market. In this chapter I will mention some of the strategies that I have found helpful, and that might be useful to you.

When I was a little boy, my grandmother used to arrange four-leafed clover hunts. The object of the game was to see who could pick the most four-leafed clovers. (I might add that a four-leafed clover is bloody hard to find, and Granny could spot one at about thirty paces.) Although I had keen eyesight and I was closer to the ground than my older brothers, they were able to snatch four-leafed clovers from right under my nose. The reason they always won was that they concentrated on the task at hand, while I let my attention be distracted by other flora and fauna (such as a dandelion or a wandering beetle). Had I kept my mind on looking for four-leafed clovers, I too would have been a winner.

I make this confession to illustrate a fundamental investment maxim: If you want to be successful, you must have a goal—and you must stick to it. If your investment goal is capital gain don't be distracted by income securities, but concentrate on equities. If your goal is income, don't get involved in speculative situations, stay with high yielding securities. If you want a combination of growth and income, then build a balanced portfolio, and keep it balanced.

This may sound elementary, but over the years I have had many people come to me who had no clear idea of what they wanted from their investments. In most cases their holdings had simply drifted with the market, rather like flotsam and jetsam that rises and falls with the economic tide. I repeat, if you want above average performance from your investments you must establish your goal, set your course, and steadfastly follow it.

Buying new issues *indiscriminately* is a good way to turn a portfolio into a hodge podge. Every new issue—at least in the eyes of the underwriter—has selling points. But what you must ask yourself, is whether the security fits into your overall plan. For instance, if you're concentrating on capital growth, you don't want a bond or even a retractable preferred, no matter how high the yield. By the same token, if you're primarily interested in income, a concept stock would not be appropriate for your needs. A new issue may not even be suitable for a balanced portfolio (one that has both growth and income securities) because it would duplicate a holding or overweight one section.

Ideally, your broker should screen new issues and only offer you those that he feels would fit into your portfolio. Even then, you must exercise judgement as to what you will buy. If you have a good business relationship with your broker, it won't hurt it if you decline his offering. (I get turned down by some of my best clients occasionally, which I think is perfectly fair.)

Should you get a call from a broker you don't know, be extremely wary. Normally, if it's a good new issue, it is *always* sold to existing clients—not telephone prospects. When an issue isn't moving well and buyers are scarce, some brokers resort to "cold" calling. That's why I say to be wary of a new issue offering from a broker who is a stranger.

On the subject of new issues, if you are offered new Canada bonds after 10:00 a.m. you would be well advised to pass them up. The reason is that Canada bonds are usually priced at 9:00 a.m. and if the issue is "hot" or even mildly warm, the *entire* issue is sold in the next fifteen minutes. Unless your favourite broker has held some back for you, an offering after 10:00 a.m.

means that the issue is going very slowly and may already be trading *below* the issue price.

Some people buy new issues with no intention of paying for them. Their plan is to realize a profit between the issue date and the settlement date. This practice is known as "riding" and is severely frowned upon in the business, although some salesmen (to generate commissions) encourage clients to ride new issues. I do *not* recommend riding, but I will tell you how to take advantage of riders. If you want to buy a "hot" issue and can't get any from your broker, the time to buy the issue in the aftermarket is just before the settlement date. It is during these last hectic days that most of the riders are forced to sell their positions. As a result, if there's a big speculative interest, a lot of shares will be dumped which will temporarily depress the price—permitting you to buy at an artificially low level.

I would also caution you about Secondary Issues. The first thing to establish is why the offering is being made. Is it a "bailout" on the part of "insiders" or is there a plausable reason (such as a forced divestiture of a subsidiary interest)? Regardless of the motive, the price of the shares will *probably decline* after the issue. The reason for the subsequent decline is that the offering will likely sop up all the available buying interest. This doesn't always happen, but it happens in the majority of cases. The only justification for buying a Secondary Issue is if you have had your eye on the stock for some time, and the price is right.

You should never buy a mutual fund without first reading the prospectus. Among the things to look for in the prospectus is the length of service of the fund managers, which will tell you whether the same team that was responsible for the previous performance is still running the show. Check on how long it takes to have shares redeemed, and find out if the shares can be transferred into another fund. (AGF, Guardian, and Investors are some of the large companies that have "families" of funds.) The right to transfer shares from one type of fund into another, *at minimal cost*, is a valuable option. To make an informed decision, you should always compare several funds.

Building a balanced portfolio is the same as building a house. First, you must have a solid foundation. For the average investor, the "foundation" should be something that is safe and liquid such as some Canada Savings Bonds or Treasury Bills. (Both provide an excellent cash reserve in case of an emergency, or for future purchases.) Having established a secure foundation, you might then buy some convertible bonds or convertible preferreds. These securities combine safety, yield, and an equity exposure. Once you have a cash reserve and some defensive investments in hand, you can concentrate on common stocks. I would stick to proven companies, and I would be extremely selective.

You would be wise to diversify by investing in a number of industries. But don't over diversify—buy one, or at the most, two companies in a given industry. After you've got a reasonable representation (say a total of ten stocks) add to your *existing* stocks rather than buying new ones. The secret to dynamic performance is to have *meaningful* holdings in the *leading* companies in each industry. If you have a grab bag of a little of this and a little of that, I can assure you that your results will be mediocre at best.

I encountered an astonishing example of over-diversification a few years ago when a dear little old lady named Florence came in to see me for advice. I told Florence that I could only be of help if she would tell me her holdings. She couldn't remember what she held, and she didn't have a list, but she said she would get her securities out of the bank and return later. The next day Florence tottered into my office lugging a huge Steinberg's shopping bag. I assumed that she had just bought her week's groceries, but I was wrong. The bag was filled with stock certificates. There wasn't enough space on my desk so I emptied the bag on the floor, got down on my hand and knees and ploughed through the paper. I found all sorts of things including companies that were no longer in existence, companies that had changed their names, companies that had split their shares, a few that had offered to redeem their shares, and a number that had been taken over by other companies. The certificates in the pile represented everything from a fraction of one share to more than six hundred shares.

After getting research opinions, I set aside her best stocks and sold everything else. The proceeds from the sales were used to bolster her remaining holdings. When the dust settled, Florence ended up with significant positions in ten companies. Streamlining her portfolio has improved its performance and for the first time in years, Florence is able to keep track of her investments. As one of my Nova Scotia friends would say, now she knows where she's at.

There are two systematic ways to add to your stock holdings. One is by "dollar averaging," the other by subscribing to a dividend re-investment plan.

The "dollar averaging" method is very simple. To do this you set aside a fixed sum on a regular basis—every quarter or every year—and buy shares in the company. Because the amount is fixed, you buy more shares when the price is low and fewer shares when the price is high. Over a period of time, you will accumulate stock at a relatively low average price. Here is an example of how it works, using a figure of $1000 for each purchase:

	Stock Price	Number of Shares Bought
1st purchase	22	($1000 ÷ $22) = 45 shares
2nd purchase	27	($1000 ÷ $27) = 37 shares
3rd purchase	33	($1000 ÷ $33) = 30 shares
4th purchase	30	($1000 ÷ $30) = 33 shares

Average purchase price 27½

Dividend re-investment plans work on the same principle. Each quarter the company buys shares for you instead of sending you your dividend in cash. Invariably the company will save you money, either in commission fees or by selling you shares from the treasury at a discount. Most of the blue chip companies, including Bell, have dividend re-investment plans. It need hardly be mentioned that if you need income, you shouldn't subscribe to this type of plan.

For those who depend upon their investments for income, you should watch the dividend and interest payment dates. As you know, common and preferred shares normally pay their dividends quarterly, while bonds usually pay interest twice a year. (Canada Savings Bonds pay interest once a year, in November.) With a little planning, you can arrange your holdings so that you receive a similar amount of income each month.

As a simple example, let us say that your portfolio consists of:

$10,000 Canada Savings Bonds paying 10% interest
1000 shares Hudson's Bay $2.25 exchangeable preferred
1000 shares Bell Enterprises common
1000 shares Bank of Montreal common

Here is a schedule of your dividends and interest:

Bell Enterprises ....
    January, April, July, and October.....................$545
Bank of Montreal..
    February, May, August, and November..............$490
Hudson's Bay ....
    March, June, September and December $562
Canada Savings Bond interest........November.......$1000

As you can see from this example, it's easy to stagger your dividend payments so that you get similar cheques each month. (The Canada Savings Bonds, which are the cash reserve in the portfolio, pay their interest when it's most needed—just before Christmas.)

If you depend upon your dividend income and are worried about the market, there is no need to sell your shares. You can protect the value of your holdings and maintain your flow of dividends by writing or buying options. If you write (sell) covered call options, the money you receive will help to offset a decline in the value of the shares. Writing calls gives you a guaranteed return, but will not compensate for a severe drop in stock prices. Also, if you judge the market incorrectly, your calls will be exercised and you will lose the stock. Therefore when writing calls, strive for the highest strike price combined with the shortest maturity—and only sell calls if you are satisfied to lose your stock at the strike price (plus the option premium).

Buying puts is exactly like buying insurance, even to the cost of the premium. Like insurance, there's no payoff unless your stock goes down in price. If this happens you have two alternatives: to sell the puts at a profit, (which will largely offset the decline in the stock, minus the premium) or exercise your right to sell the shares at the strike price of the puts. The disadvantage to puts is that often the premium makes them a prohibitively expensive form of insurance. For this reason you should always calculate the cost of the put premium against the expected decline in the stock.

If, for instance, you held a stock that was trading at 29 and you thought it could fall to 25, you might consider buying puts with a 27½ strike price. This would make sense if you could buy the puts for 50 or 75 cents but not if you had to pay two dollars for the puts. Here is the calculation, excluding commission:

Strike Price of puts		Cost of Premium		Net Proceeds	Theoretical Profit
$27½	minus	.50	=	$27.00	$2.00
$27½	minus	.75	=	$26.75	$1.75
$27½	minus	$2.00	=	$25.50	50

This strategy applies to the protection of a single security, and can only be done if there are options outstanding on that security. If you want to protect your entire portfolio (which may consist of stocks that do not have options) you can take advantage of the same strategy by selling calls or buying puts on the TSE 300 Composite Index. It should be mentioned that the value of your holdings will probably *not* move in lock step with the Composite Index, (because the make-up of your portfolio is different from the TSE 300), therefore you will not get dollar for dollar coverage. You can also achieve the same type of hedge in the futures market, based on the TSE Composite Index, but I would not recommend this for the average investor.

Harking back to the section on technical analysis, you should try to buy puts or write calls near a resistance level, and you should try to buy calls or write puts near a support level. The logic behind these recommendations is obvious (providing you've read the previous chapter).

Options are also useful for tax purposes. Suppose you have a large capital gain in a stock, but you can't afford to sell it in the present year. At the same time, you are worried that the stock may decline between now and next year. To protect your profit you hedge your position by buying puts that expire next year. Even if the stock goes down in the interim, you will have locked in most of your gain.

The reverse of this situation is when you want to sell a loser for tax purposes, but you are afraid the stock may go up sharply before you are allowed to repurchase it. (If you sell a stock for a tax loss, the loss will be disallowed if you repurchase the same stock within thirty days of the sale.) To get around this problem, you buy calls on the stock and this assures you a fixed repurchase cost, or a profit on the calls, if the shares should go through the roof.

Options are often used to trigger a loss in the current year, and to shift a capital gain into the next year by means of a "straddle." (A straddle is the simultaneous purchase or sale of a put and a call on the same security, with the same strike price and the same expiry date.) The losing "leg" of the straddle is liquidated in the present year, while the profitable "leg" is liquidated in the new year. *This form of tax deferral may be disallowed by Revenue Canada and should only be attempted after consulting your tax advisor.*

Another type of hedging strategy involves the purchase of convertible bonds on margin, and the short sale of the underlying shares. This is perfectly legal, and has been done by the financial community and the public for years. Ideally, the shares should be volatile, and the bonds should be trading below par with very little premium attached to the underlying stock. The rationale behind this transaction is that the convertible bonds (being a senior security) will fall less than the common shares which you have sold short. When the stock declines sufficiently, you cover your short sale by simply buying the shares back on the open market. The profit on the short sale more than makes up for the "paper" loss on the bonds. If the stock should go up, the bonds will also increase in value by a similar amount, and if you are forced to cover your short position you can make delivery by converting your bonds into stock. The worst scenario is when the price of the common remains stable. In this case your carrying costs—margin charges and payment of any dividends on the shorted shares—can put you into a loss position.

This hedging strategy may sound confusing, so I'll give you a theoretical example. Let's assume that you paid ninety-eight for a bond that's convertible into one hundred common shares. You short the shares at ten dollars and cover the short at five dollars. Here are the figures:

```
Proceeds received from short sale (100 × $10)  = $1000
            Cost to cover short sale (100 × $5)  = $  500
                          Profit on short sale              $500
               Cost of convertible bond @ 98  = $  980
               Bond declines in value to 75  = $  750
                                 Loss on bond              $230
        Net profit on transaction ($500 – $230)  = $270
```

Because the choice of convertible bonds is limited in Canada, the best market is in the United States. For those of you who are interested in convertible hedging and would like to learn more about it, you might read *The New Profit Taker*, by Don Abrams, which is published by Deneau. This book contains a sophisticated variation of the convertible hedging technique.

Now let's turn to "straight" bonds. Many investors are faced with the problem of holding long term bonds that are trading at a discount. They consider themselves to be "locked-in" because if they sell the bonds now they will realize a substantial loss. Unless interest rates drop, they will have to wait until the bonds mature to get their money back. Fortunately, there is a way out of this bind—if you're willing to accept a *smaller amount of annual income*. You trade your long term bonds for short term bonds with a lower coupon. At this writing, if you held Government of Canada thirteen per cent due in 2001 you could trade them for Government of Canada ten per cent due in 1986, *without putting up any money*. As a result of this switch, your annual income would drop from $130 per year for each $1000 bond to $100 per year, but you'd get your money back in *two years* rather than having to wait for seventeen years.

This strategy can be employed in reverse, if you want to

increase your annual income. You can easily switch from a low coupon near term maturity to a high coupon long term bond. Supposing you held Government of Canada 10¾% due in 1985. You could swap these bonds for Government of Canada 13½% due in 1999 and take a few dollars out on the way through. This transaction would increase your income per $1000 bond from $107.50 to $135.00 per year. However, in view of the trend in interest rates over the past thirty years I would *not* recommend lengthening maturities—the risk is not worth the reward. In fact, I would suggest that you make an orderly retreat from the long end of the bond market by *shortening* terms.

Having looked at the serious side of investing, I would like to make a few observations on the lighter side—the junior resource stocks. Some of the penny dreadfuls have substantial intrinsic value in the form of wealth in the ground, but due to low metal prices are uneconomic to bring into production. If you sniff these situations out, and you are prepared to wait a few years for your pay-off, you can make very big profits. The way to find junior stocks with this type of value is to study the *Handbook of Mines* published by *The Northern Miner*, or the *Survey of Mines and Energy Resources* which is published by *The Financial Post*.

One of my clients, Adam, is a successful lawyer with a knowledge of the mining game and an excellent sense of humour. Adam is a "gold bug" and he loves to speculate. Because I like to keep my clients solvent, I often have to restrain Adam's enthusiasm for some of the high flying Vancouver stocks. (In fact, I think I spend more time telling him *not* to buy than encouraging him to trade.) A few years ago, when the price of gold was hitting new lows, Adam asked me for a copy of the *Handbook of Mines*. When I sent him the book I wrote in the covering note that I felt as though I was handing a pyromaniac a box of matches. I didn't hear from him for ten days or so, and then he phoned to give me a batch of buy orders. Most of the names I had never heard before, and all were low priced gold mines—but as I later found out they all had intrinsic value. The price of gold eventually firmed, and about eighteen months later Adam sold these stocks for two or three times what he had paid for them. He deserved this bonanza, because he had done his homework, and he had waited for the cyclical recovery in the price of gold.

If you are an impatient sort who wants action, and don't care to do any research, you might try "tape hopping." This is an old speculative technique that evolved in the days when brokerage houses projected the ticker tape on a screen for the benefit of their customers. The ticker tape is still very much in use, but nowadays there are few "boardrooms" for customers, and the brokers watch the tape on personal video screens. Regardless of how the tape is watched, it tells a story because it continually relays news from the floor of the exchange. Information on the tape is transmitted by means of symbols and numbers—the symbols stand for the names of the stocks and the numbers indicate prices and volume. This is what a section of the tape looks like:

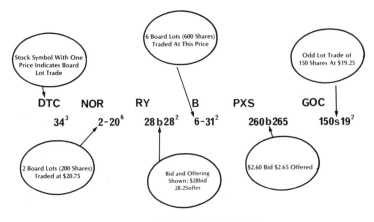

TICKER TAPE SYMBOLS

As you can well imagine, if you're interested in the market, watching the tape can be a fascinating pastime. When I worked for Bongard & Co. we had a boardroom which was filled with spectators all day. Many of them, seeing a particular stock become active and start to move would buy it blind on the premise that it was going higher. These were "tape hoppers" and quite frequently they made money by darting in and out of the stock. I had one client who used to give me buy orders by telling me the stock's symbol—not even knowing the name of the stock, let alone the prospects of the company. Being well aware that the tape is closely watched, promoters sometimes "paint the tape" to create the impression that there is heavy buying in a stock, which of course will attract the tape hoppers. Painting the tape is done by dribbling a lot of little orders through the exchange at one time. Let us suppose that the mythical Old Moose Pasture Mines (whose symbol is OMP) is being given a "run" and the promoter is painting the tape. Here's how it might look:

OMP	OMP	OMP	XYZ	OMP
$5 - 2^2$	$3 - 2^2$	$2 - 2^2$	$4^2b - 4^3$	$3 - 2$

A PAINTED TAPE

Painting the tape still sucks in buyers because brokers watch their video screens closely, and when they see a stock become active they often phone their clients. If you want to make money on this type of a gamble the secret is to buy it on the *first* day of the "run" and to sell it no later than the *third* day. The reason for this short cycle is that many penny dreadfuls—particularly on the Vancouver Exchange—surge on the basis of a rumour and then collapse. Tape hopping is a *very dangerous game*, and should not be confused with investing.

On the subject of speculative stocks, many investors are comforted if they know their broker owns the stock himself. This is false logic. If you own a stock, it is human nature to expect the best possible outcome and to recommend it to your friends. A broker that owns a stock may think he has "inside information" but at the same time he can't be objective about it. For this reason I rarely buy a penny dreadful for my own account, and when I do I warn my clients that it is probably the kiss of death. And it usually is.

It is also a truism that most investors think they have to be in the market all the time. Often, the *smartest* move you can make is to withdraw your money from the market and to sit on the sidelines. While you're taking a breather your money can be earning a return in Treasury Bills or a short term deposit account.

(Brokerage firms usually pay competitive rates on credit balances.)

When investors want to raise money—for whatever purpose—they frequently sell their winners. I can't tell you how many times I have had clients look over their holdings and then make this horrendous error. What you should do is keep your winners and *sell your losers*. You might liken this approach to owning a woodlot. If you needed firewood would you cut down the healthy trees, or would you cull out the dead ones? Obviously if you kept cutting down the healthy trees, you'd eventually have a woodlot consisting of dead trees. By the same token, if you persist in selling your winning investments and keeping your losers, you will end up with a portfolio of garbage.

The best market advice I ever received was given to me by a client named Lazarus, who for many years owned a seat on the New York Stock Exchange. He was an extraordinarily shrewd trader and had made a fortune in the market. The last time I visited him in New York, which was shortly before his death, he took me to lunch at the Bankers' Club. At the end of our lunch, I asked him what was the most valuable lesson he had learned in his years on Wall Street. He thought the question over and then replied:

"Take your losses quickly, and let your profits run."

To close this book I can't think of any better advice to leave with you. I would only add that I hope your losses will be trivial and your profits glorious!

END

ACKNOWLEDGEMENTS

FOR THE BEST PART of four years my friend and colleague, Rick Southee, nagged me to write this book. Therefore he is the first I must thank—or blame—for *The Money Labyrinth*. I was also helped in various ways by other friends, and among those I would especially like to thank: Tom Banks, Deans Berry, Roland Bertin, Don Betts, Tim Boreham, Mary Cassidy, Doug Cameron, Paula Dunlap, Alan Ferry, Dick Fraser, Mimi Fullerton, Lloyd Garrett, John Gillelan, John Gilmour, Alex Gluskin, Gordon Harris, Joe Irvin, Paul Joseph, Anne Morrison, Karen Nonnenkamp, Bob Parsons, Jean-Charles Potvin, Reddy Quain, Ann Rait, David Scott, Fred Stanton, Doug Tuck, and Silvester von Herrman.

I am indebted to Art Moody and Larry Esmonde-White of the Canadian Bank Note Company for their assistance in obtaining reproductions of the share certificates used in this book—and to Lumonics Inc., Victoria and Grey Trust, and the Bank of Nova Scotia for permission to use them. I would also like to thank the Bank of Canada for permission to reproduce the facsimile of a Canada Savings Bond.

Sue Nelson of Burns Fry drew the diagrams and graphs that appear in the text. I am most grateful to Sue for the time and trouble she took to accomodate me on this project. I should also acknowledge that Burns Fry permitted me to print some of the firm's charts and the "tombstone" on Occidental Petroleum.

Whit Tucker, the resident director of Burns Fry in Ottawa,

deserves special mention because he not only made some excellent suggestions for the book, but he kept a stiff upper lip while my production sagged during the months I was writing it.

Both the jacket photo and two other illustrations were done by my old friend, Michael Heney.

The Money Labyrinth might not have become a reality had it not been for my former editor, Janet Turnbull, who shepherded the manuscript through the critical early stages, and saw that I was firmly launched before she moved on to another senior position in the publishing industry.

Finally, I want to thank my favourite client—my wife Sandrea—who has vetted every word of the manuscript and given me a lot of good advice. For this she has earned my heartfelt gratitude, and possibly a candle-lit dinner at an expensive restaurant.

GLOSSARY

ACCOUNT EXECUTIVE—pretentious title for a REGISTERED REPRESENTATIVE, BROKER, or Salesman.

ACCRUED INTEREST—interest on a bond that has accumulated from the last payment date. When you buy a bond you pay for the accrued interest; when you sell a bond you receive accrued interest. A bond without accrued interest is said to be trading "flat."

ACID-TEST RATIO—used to measure liquidity of a company. To get this figure deduct inventory from current assets and divide remainder by current liabilities.

AGENT—Broker that does not own the security but simply buys or sells it for the client and receives a fee (commission) for his services. Most stock exchange trades are done this way.

ALLIGATOR SPREAD—an option spread that costs the client more in commission than his potential profit. Should be avoided.

ADR—an ADR or American Depository Receipt is a certificate of ownership of a foreign security, held in an offshore branch of an American bank. Most South African gold mining shares traded in North America are ADRs.

AMEX—Also known as the ASE, stands for the American Stock Exchange which is the second largest in the United States.

Located in New York, the AMEX trades a lot of the "swingers" and junior stocks as well as bonds and options.

ANNUITY—an investment contract issued by an insurance company for a lump sum that pays you a fixed amount at regular periods for the length of your life or until you reach a certain age.

ARBITRAGE—a strategy used by professionals whereby a security is bought or sold on one market to profit from a price difference in another market.

ASSIGN—when an option is exercised you are assigned the security which means you must deliver the shares or buy them, depending whether you have sold (written) calls or puts.

AVERAGE DOWN—a strategy to reduce the cost of a security by buying more as the price declines. Unrewarding if the stock goes into the tank.

BALANCE SHEET—a financial statement that shows a company's assets, liabilities, and net worth.

BANK OF CANADA—established in 1934. Regulates credit and currency of the nation and controls external value of Canadian dollar. Sole issuer of currency, and custodian of Canada's gold reserves.

BASIS POINT—usually applied to yields, represents one one hundredth of one per cent. If a yield rises from 12.20% to 12.30% the change is 10 basis points.

BEAR—one who believes a security or the market will decline.

BEAR RAID—concerted attack on a stock with the object of forcing down the price by means of short sales. The bears often have a field day on the Vancouver Exchange.

BETA—an indication of a stock's volatility in relation to an index such as the TSE300 or Standard & Poor's 500. Excellent word to drop at a cocktail party, because it implies both a knowledge of the market and of Greek.

BLOCK—when applied to the market refers to a stock transaction of 10,000 or more shares with a value in excess of $200,000.

BLUE CHIP—a large company that is a leader in its industry with a consistent record of earnings and dividends.

BLUE-SKY—to get legal clearance for the sale of a new issue in all of the provinces (or states).

BOILER ROOM—where stock hustlers work the telephones to push speculative (and often worthless) securities.

BOND—a debt security backed by a pledge of assets. See also DEBENTURE.

BOOK VALUE—total tangible assets minus all liabilities and the par value of all preferred shares. Divide the number of common shares into this figure to get book value per share.

BROAD TAPE—nickname for Dow Jones news service.

BROKER—can mean an individual or a firm in the securities business. See AGENT and ACCOUNT EXECUTIVE.

CAGE—section of brokers office where securities are physically handled. Called a cage because the area used to be enclosed by wire walls to prevent theft. Harried cage employees sometimes act as though they are occupants of a zoo.

CALL OPTION—a security that gives you the right to buy the shares of a company at a fixed price for a fixed period of time.

CALLABLE—security that can be redeemed before the maturity date at the option of the issuer.

CHARTIST—one who uses a technical approach to security analysis and relies upon stock charts to forecast prices.

CHICAGO BOARD OF TRADE—oldest and largest commodity exchange in North America. Also trades currencies and financial futures. Parent of CBOE or Chicago Board Options Exchange, North America's largest option market.

CHICAGO MERCANTILE EXCHANGE—second largest commodity exchange in North America. Parent of International Monetary Market.

CHURNING—excessive trading of a client's account to generate commissions. Unless there is evidence that the broker prompted the trades *and* the client has lost money, churning is difficult to prove.

COMEX—commodity exchange located in New York. Main market in North America for precious metals and financial instruments.

COMMON STOCK—represents the equity or ownership of a company. Normally, common shareholders have voting rights and by this means control the management of the company.

CONVERTIBLE—usually refers to bonds or preferred shares that may be converted into common shares of the company.

COOP—stands for Conventional Old Oil Price, which applies to oil discovered in Canada before 1 April 1974. Under the terms of the National Energy Policy this oil is sold for approximately 75 percent of the world oil price.

COUPON—the interest rate expressed as a percentage of the face value of a debt security, e.g., a 6 percent coupon on a bond. Also refers to small cashable certificates attached to a bond representing interest instalments.

CURRENT RATIO—arrived at by dividing the current liabilities of a company into its current assets. If a company has current liabilities of $1 million and current assets of $3 million this would give a 3 to 1 current ratio.

DEBENTURE—a form of long term debt, similar to a bond, that is not secured by specific assets but by the general credit of the issuer.

DEBT/EQUITY RATIO—usually calculated by adding total long term debt plus preferred shares and dividing common shareholders' equity into this amount. Indicates earnings leverage in corporate structure.

DEPLETION—accounting allowance for amount of ore or oil that is withdrawn (used up) from a mine or oil well.

DEPRECIATION—accounting allowance or reserve that represents the loss of value of an asset (such as a factory), through wear and tear or obsolescence. The value of the asset is written down on the company's books by this amount each year.

DISCRETIONARY ACCOUNT—an account where the client gives the broker *written* authority to make investment decisions on behalf of the client. Should only be done after careful consideration of the consequences.

DIVIDEND—cash distribution, usually on a quarterly basis, to common and preferred shareholders made at the discretion of the board of directors.

DIVIDEND TAX CREDIT—applicable to dividends on shares of Canadian companies. Canadian residents "gross-up" and report 150% of the amount of the dividend, and then deduct 34% of that sum from Federal Tax Payable.

DOUBLE PLAY—an investment opportunity that has two separate profit potentials e.g., a Japanese stock that may appreciate in value, and may also be worth more in Canadian dollars because of an increase in the exchange rate for the yen.

DOW JONES INDUSTRIAL AVERAGE—a measurement of market movement based on the changing values of thirty senior stocks listed on the New York Stock Exchange. The most widely followed stock index in the financial world.

EARNINGS PER SHARE—often expressed as EPS, this is calculated by dividing the number of common shares into the net income (after taxes and dividends on the preferred) of the company. An important statistic when analysing the value of a stock.

EURODOLLARS—U.S. dollars held in Europe. When used to pay for oil they become PETRODOLLARS. If used to pay for American goods they return to the U.S. as regular Yankee dollars. But so long as they circulate offshore they are EURODOLLARS.

FANNIE MAE—nickname for the Federal National Mortgage Association. Debt securities issued by this American agency are known as "Fannie Maes."

GO-GO FUNDS—mutual funds with speculative portfolios that are supposed to give superior performance. Time has not been kind to them.

GOVERNMENT NATIONAL MORTGAGE ASSOCIATION—a U.S. federal corporation whose securities have been nick-named "Ginnie Maes."

GREEN SHOE—a provision that permits the underwriter to draw down additional securities and thereby expand the size of an issue. Useful if the underwriter is short the issue, or if an unexpected demand develops for the issue.

GROSS PRODUCTION—a resource company's production before payment of royalties.

I.D.A.—stands for Investment Dealers Association of Canada, which was founded in 1916. National self-regulatory body for Canadian securities industry.

INSIDER—one who owns more than ten per cent of a company's stock, or who is a senior officer of the company. Also applies to a person with "inside" information.

INSTITUTIONAL INVESTOR—industry term for large investors such as insurance companies, trust companies, mutual funds, and banks.

INTEGRATED OIL—refers to vertical integration of an oil company that does everything, from exploration through to the sale of the refined products at its own gas stations.

KICKER—a special feature added to an otherwise bland security (such as a bond) to make it attractive to investors. The KICKER might be anything from a retraction privilege to free warrants to buy the company's common shares.

LATE TAPE—indicates that trading is so hectic on the exchange that transactions are being reported late on the ticker tape.

LEVERAGE—using a small amount of money to get the play off a larger amount. Securities bought on margin are a good example of leverage.

LIBOR—stands for London Interbank Offered Rate. Only of interest to major institutions and large investors.

LIFTING A LEG—when applied to securities, refers to removal of one side of a hedge. Has entirely different connotation when applied to dogs.

LIQUIDITY—the ability of a security to be converted quickly into cash. Also referred to as marketability. Highly desirable.

MARGIN—can mean either the client's equity in a securities account, or the purchase of securities with the aid of money loaned by the broker.

MARGIN CALL—what the broker issues when your equity falls below the minimum requirement in a margin account. You respond to a margin call by putting up more money (or securities) or by selling some of your position. If you do not respond, the broker can sell you out.

NAKED WRITER—a person who sells call options on stock he does not own, or who sells put options when he is not short the stock (or is not long an offsetting put).

NATIONAL ENERGY POLICY—government policy designed to conserve Canada's oil and gas supply, and to make the country self sufficient. Production and pricing of oil and gas are regulated by federal and provincial authorities under this policy.

NET WORTH—the amount a company's assets exceed its liabilities. Also called SHAREHOLDERS' EQUITY.

NEW YORK STOCK EXCHANGE—founded in 1792. The largest and best known securities market in North America. Most of the issues listed on the NYSE are "blue chips" or senior companies.

NIFTY FIFTY—a term used to describe the fifty favourite stocks of the American institutions. Came into vogue in the 1970s but infrequently heard today.

NORP—stands for New Oil Reference Price, which applies to oil discovered in Canada after 1 April 1974. NORP oil is sold for approximately the world price.

OPTION—in securities parlance, refers to calls or puts. Call options give you the *right* to buy the underlying stock at a fixed price for a fixed period of time. Put options allow you to sell the underlying stock under the same conditions. Selling calls or puts (which is known as "writing") places an *obligation* on the vendor to deliver or to buy the underlying stock if the options are exercised.

OVER-THE-COUNTER—a securities market where dealers trade among themselves by telephone or telex rather than by open outcry on a stock exchange.

PAPER PROFIT—the profit in a security that has not been liquidated. The opposite is of course a "paper loss."

PAR VALUE—the face value of a bond upon maturity, or the price at which preferred shares may be redeemed (unless there is a premium). Usually meaningless when applied to common shares.

PETROLEUM INCENTIVE PAYMENTS—can cover as much as eighty per cent of Canadian frontier exploration costs. Higher for Canadian companies than foreign companies. Also called PIP grants.

POINT—with reference to stocks, it means a dollar move, e.g., Alcan moved up a point from thirty-five dollars to thirty-six dollars. With regard to bonds, it can either mean a one per cent move on the face value of a bond, or one hundred basis points in yield.

PREFERRED SHARE—equity in a company that ranks ahead of the common shares. Preferred shares normally have a par value, and usually do not participate in the earnings except to the extent of a fixed dividend rate. Often called "preference" shares.

PRICE/EARNINGS RATIO—to calculate this ratio divide the earnings per share into the price of the stock. If a stock is trading at thirty dollars and the EPS are three dollars, the stock is selling at ten times earnings or a PRICE/EARNINGS ratio of ten to one.

PRIME RATE—in Canada the Bank Rate (the rate the Bank of Canada will lend money to the chartered banks) is set at twenty five basis points above the average yield of ninety-one Day Treasury Bills, which are auctioned every Thursday. In turn, the chartered banks set their Prime Rate—the rate they will lend money to their best customers—at a full point or so above the Bank Rate.

PRO FORMA—a Latin phrase meaning "according to custom" which is used to describe financial projections in a prospectus which show the effect of the proceeds of the issue on the balance sheet.

PROSPECTUS—a document or brochure that gives relevant information concerning a new issue. Contents of a prospectus must conform to strict legal requirements. Tedious but important reading for prospective purchaser.

PROVEN RESERVES—amount of oil, gas, or ore that has been established by drilling, and that can be extracted by present technology.

PUT OPTION—security that gives you the right to sell a given number of shares at a fixed price for a fixed period of time.

RED HERRING—industry nickname for a preliminary prospectus.

REGISTERED REPRESENTATIVE—correct name for a licenced securities salesman. See also ACCOUNT EXECUTIVE.

RIGHT OF RESCISSION—legal right to cancel purchase of a new securities issue if it has been misrepresented in the prospectus.

RIGHTS OFFERING—privilege extended to existing common shareholders which permits them to buy additional shares in the company, on a pro rata basis, at a discount from the current price. If a shareholder doesn't want to take advantage of the offer, the "rights" usually have value and can be sold on the market.

ROLLOVER—usually applies to the reinvestment of funds, e.g., when a Treasury Bill matures the money is "rolled over" into another Treasury Bill.

SECONDARY OFFERING—the sale of a block of securities to the public by an existing holder. The money goes to the vendor, not into the treasury of the company. Sometimes a secondary is a "bailout" by the vendor. For this reason, SECONDARY OFFERINGS should be viewed with caution.

SECURITIES AND EXCHANGE COMMISSION—established in 1934. Federal Agency that is responsible for enforcement of securities regulations in the United States. Usually referred to as the SEC.

SELLING GROUP—investment dealers who participate in an underwriting as sales agents, but are not members of the underwriting syndicate.

SHARE—a piece of the action, or more properly an equity unit in a company. See COMMON STOCK.

SHORT—the sale of securities that the client borrows from the broker. If and when the shorted securities fall in value, they are bought back or "covered" by the client. The difference between the sale price and the purchase price is the client's profit (or loss).

SINKING FUND—does not refer to a poorly performing mutual fund, but to money set aside by a corporation for the repurchase of a portion of its outstanding bonds or preferred shares.

SOUR GAS—natural gas that is contaminated with sulphur. The sulphur must be removed before the gas can be used for industrial or domestic purposes.

SPREAD—the simultaneous purchase and sale of options of the same class to benefit from a change in price of the underlying stock. Both the risk and the reward are limited in a spread. Term is also used to describe a similar strategy in trading commodities.

STANDARD & POOR'S—well known American financial service.

STOCK DIVIDEND—distribution by company of treasury shares in lieu of a cash dividend.

STRADDLE—in option trading refers to the simultaneous purchase or sale of a call and a put on a stock with the same strike price and the same expiration date.

STREET—in its purest sense, Wall Street, New York. Now used to refer to the financial community in general.

STRIKE PRICE—the price at which an option may be exercised, e.g, a call option with a strike price of thirty dollars gives you the right to buy the underlying stock at that price.

SWEETENER—industry slang for a feature that makes a mundane new issue more attractive to buyers. See KICKER.

SYNDICATE—a group of investment dealers who underwrite a new securities issue. A syndicate buys the entire issue, and is responsible for marketing the issue at a set price.

TAILGATING—when a registered representative executes an order for a well-informed client, and then buys the same security for his own account. A rather innocuous and sometimes futile practice.

TAKE THE GAS—unpleasant consequence of owning a security that falls dramatically in price. See TURKEY.

THRIFT INSTITUTION—slang term for a bank, trust company, credit union or Caisse Populaire.

TICKER—the mechanism that relays and displays transactions from the floor of the stock exchanges.

TOMBSTONE—industry nickname for the advertisement of a new securities issue. Names on the tombstone are ranked in order of precedence (as to their participation) from the top down.

TRADING PIT—a raised, octagonal-shaped platform with descending steps on the inside where futures are traded.

TRANSFER AGENT—an institution, normally a trust company, that is responsible for the issuance and cancellation of bond and stock certificates. Each company has its own particular transfer agent, e.g., Bell Telephone uses the Royal Trust.

TREASURY BILL—a short term obligation of the Government of Canada. Most T Bills are issued for a term of ninety-one days but they can have a term of up to two years. They do not bear interest. Their yield comes from the difference between the discount at which they are purchased and their face value at maturity.

TURKEY—a security whose price movement causes profound distress to the holder.

UNDERWRITE—the purchase by one or more investment dealers of a securities issue. Until the issue is sold to the public, the underwriters are normally at risk for the entire amount of the issue.

UNIT—a securities issue that consists of more than one component, e.g., a stock issue that includes a share purchase warrant with each common share.

VARIABLE RATE—a bond or preferred share that does not have a fixed rate of return, but pays interest or dividends based on prevailing interest rates. These securities use different formulae to establish their variable rates.

WARRANT—has two meanings; either a long term right to purchase shares, or a certificate for rights.

WATERED STOCK—the issuance of additional shares without any money going into the treasury of the company. Dilutes the equity of existing shareholders, hence the term WATERED STOCK.

WHITE KNIGHT—a person or a corporation that averts an unfriendly takeover by making a better bid for the shares of the target company.

WIRE HOUSE—a term for a large brokerage firm with numerous

branches. These firms maintain an elaborate communications network with their branch offices.

WORKING CAPITAL—the amount remaining after current liabilities are deducted from the current assets of a company.

WRITE—when applied to options, means the sale of a put or a call.

YIELD—the return, expressed as a percentage, on a security.

ZERO COUPON BOND—a bond that has been stripped of its coupons. Both the stripped bond and the separate coupons are discounted and sold to investors. Because neither the bond nor the coupons pay interest, the return on the stripped bond comes from the difference between its discount and its par value at maturity. Similarly, the return on the coupons come from their discount and their face value at maturity.

INDEX

MOINS DE
100
ACTIONS
LESS THAN 100
SHARES

NUMÉRO
NUMBER

E 000000

INCORPORATED UNDER THE LAWS OF CANADA

AUTHORIZED CAPITAL STOCK $50,000,000. DIVIDED INTO 25,000,000 SHARES OF THE PAR VALUE OF $2. EACH

THE BANK OF

STRENGTH IN

THIS CERTIFIES THAT
CECI ATTESTE QUE

is the registered holder of
est détenteur enregistré de

FULLY PAID AND NON-ASSESSABLE SHARES OF THE PAR VALUE OF $2. EACH

of the capital stock of The Bank of Nova Scotia. Entry of the transfer of
shares represented by this certificate may be made only on the books of the Bank
upon surrender of this certificate with a duly executed transfer endorsed thereon
or delivered therewith. This certificate is not valid until countersigned and
registered on behalf of the Bank.

In Witness Whereof the Bank has caused this certificate to be signed by its duly
authorized officers.

A113 035946 3

SPECIMEN

CHIEF GENERAL MANAGER
GÉRANT GÉNÉRAL EN CHEF

AUTHORIZED OFFICER · OFFICIER AUTORISÉ

COUNTERSIGNED AND REGISTERED
CONTRESIGNÉ ET ENREGISTRÉ

BY
PAR

TRANSFERABLE AT ST. JOHN'S, HALIFAX, CHARLOTTETOWN, SAINT JOHN, MONTREAL, TORONTO, WINNIPEG,
REGINA, CALGARY, VANCOUVER, LONDON, ENGLAND AND NEW YORK, U.S.A.